Dan Russel The Fox: An Episode In The Life Of Miss Rowan

E. Somerville

Printing Statement:

Due to the very old age and scarcity of this book, many of the pages may be hard to read due to the blurring of the original text, possible missing pages, missing text, dark backgrounds and other issues beyond our control.

Because this is such an important and rare work, we believe it is best to reproduce this book regardless of its original condition.

Thank you for your understanding.

DAN RUSSEL THE FOX

FOX .

AN EPISODE IN THE LIFE OF
MISS ROWAN

BY

E. Œ. SOMERVILLE AND MARTIN ROSS

METHUEN & CO. LTD.
36 ESSEX STREET W.C.
LONDON

First Published, at 1s. net, in 1913

This Book was First Published . . . October 5th, 1911
Second and Third Editions . . . October 1911
Fourth Edition . . . . . . December 1911
Fifth Edition . . . . . . January 1912
Sixth Edition . . . . . . September 1912
Seventh Edition . . . . . . December 1912

Methuen's Shilling Library

A SERIES of general literature issued in fcap. 8vo. at 1s. net, printed on good paper and well bound in cloth. The books are reprints of well-known works by popular authors.

The following are either ready or in the press :—

Two Admirals	Admiral John Moresby
The Parish Clerk	P. H. Ditchfield
Thomas Henry Huxley	P. Chalmers Mitchell
Hills and the Sea	H. Belloc
Old Country Life	S. Baring-Gould
The Vicar of Morwenstow	S. Baring-Gould
Intentions	Oscar Wilde
An Ideal Husband	Oscar Wilde
Lady Windermere's Fan	Oscar Wilde
De Profundis	Oscar Wilde
Selected Poems	Oscar Wilde
Lord Arthur Savile's Crime	Oscar Wilde
A Little of Everything	E. V. Lucas
John Boyes, King of the Wa-Kikuyu	John Boyes
*Jimmy Glover—His Book	James M. Glover
Vailima Letters	Robert Louis Stevenson
Tennyson	A. C. Benson
The Blue Bird	Maurice Maeterlinck
Mary Magdalene	Maurice Maeterlinck
Sevastopol and other Stories	Leo Tolstoy
*The Life of Robert Louis Stevenson	Graham Balfour
*The Life of John Ruskin	W. G. Collingwood
The Condition of England	C. F. G. Masterman, M.P.
Letters from a Self-Made Merchant to his Son	George Horace Lorimer
The Lore of the Honey Bee	Tickner Edwardes
Under Five Reigns	Lady Dorothy Nevill
*From Midshipman to Field Marshal	Sir Evelyn Wood
Man and the Universe	Sir Oliver Lodge

* Slightly abridged

Methuen & Co., Ltd., 36, Essex Street, London, W.C.

Methuen's Shilling Novels

The following are either ready or in the press :—

Dan Russel the Fox	E. Œ. Somerville and Martin Ross
Fire in Stubble	Baroness Orczy
Splendid Brother	W. Pett Ridge
Joseph	Frank Danby
Saïd the Fisherman	Marmaduke Pickthall
Hill Rise	W. B. Maxwell
The Guarded Flame	W. B. Maxwell
The Mighty Atom	Marie Corelli
Jane	Marie Corelli
Light Freights	W. W. Jacobs
The Demon	C. N. and A. M. Williamson
Lady Betty Across the Water	C. N. and A. M. Williamson
The Tyrant	Mrs. Henry de la Pasture
Anna of the Five Towns	Arnold Bennett
The Secret Woman	Eden Phillpotts
The Long Road	John Oxenham
The Severins	Mrs. A. Sidgwick
Under the Red Robe	Stanley Weyman
Mirage	E. Temple Thurston
Virginia Perfect	Peggy Webling
Spanish Gold	G. A. Birmingham
Barbary Sheep	Robert Hichens
The Woman with the Fan	Robert Hichens
The Golden Centipede	Louise Gerard
Round the Red Lamp	Sir A. Conan Doyle
The Halo	Baroness von Hutten
Tales of Mean Streets	Arthur Morrison
The Missing Delora	E. Phillips Oppenheim
The Charm	Alice Perrin

Methuen & Co., Ltd., 36 Essex Street, London, W.C.

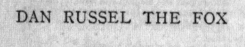

DAN RUSSEL THE FOX

Then Dan Russel the fox stert up at once,

    .   .   .   .   .

His colour was betwix yelwe and red ;
And tipped was his tail, and both his eres
With black, unlike the remenant of his heres.
His snout was smal, with glowing eyen twey ;

    .   .   .   .

A col fox, ful of sleigh iniquitee."

THE NONNES PREESTES TALE
The Canterbury Tales,
Chaucer.

DAN RUSSEL THE FOX

CHAPTER I

IT is better, when practicable, to begin at the beginning of the episode.

Katharine Rowan went to Aix-les-Bains, primarily because, at the moment, she had nothing else to do ; she went there, in the second place, because Mrs. Masterman suggested it, and moreover assured her that she would find it a thoroughly conducive place for writing ; wherein Mrs. Masterman lied.

Not intentionally, it may be admitted. Her mornings were devoted to her " cure " in its various ramifications. Doubtless, as she lay simmering in her blankets and viewed the fervent foreign sky, sandwiched between the slits of the Venetian blinds, and heard the tangled chiming of many church bells, and smelled the strange and excellent savours that ascended from the kitchen through the vine curtain of the balcony, and absorbed the sweet influences of France through every pore, she believed that the balmy leisure must be fraught with inspiration, and that the pages of foolscap were falling like snow from the pen of her young friend. It was characteristic of Mrs. Masterman's generous belief in her friends

7

that she had accepted Katharine as a writer on the strength of a report of amateur theatricals compiled by her for Captain Masterman's regimental magazine, and also because a bazaar palmist had, for the moderate sum of one shilling, promised Miss Rowan a successful literary career. Mrs. Masterman had, like Katharine, both Irish and Scotch blood in her, and the palmist had found both ladies very sympathetic. Ulick Adare had indeed predicted something to the same effect, but that, as Katharine pointed out to Mrs. Masterman, was the direct result of the letter that she had written to him about his last book.

" He asked me to criticise it, so of course I praised it. Any infant knows that if it is asked for criticism it is expected to offer adulation," said the sapient Miss Katharine ; " as a matter of fact it was excellent. All his stuff is. But he knew that as well as I did."

Yet the fact that Mr. Ulysses Adare had thought her praise worth asking for played its part in the question of the career ; and the desire for the pen, with its vain-gloriousness, its self-consciousness, its insincerity, was born.

Also its humiliations. Equipped with an MS. book, a stylograph, and a sun-umbrella, Miss Rowan strode purposefully through the public gardens of Aix, and found them swarmed over by black-pinafored children, insatiably inquisitive, and with every seat occupied by nurses, rapt in ecstasies of conversation ; she tried the basket chairs in the balconies of the " Cercle," and such people as she knew at Aix arrived, full of sociability, and disposed themselves in the surrounding chairs. She climbed, in the stupefying glare of 11 a.m., to certain wooded heights that still survive the upward march of hotels, and found that by the time she had gazed her fill at the Dent du Chat, pale with heat in the tense stillness of the midday sky, and watched through the liquid and trembling air the steamer creeping like a water-beetle across the

lake to Haute Combe, and had shaken off the hypno-
tism of the whirring grasshoppers, and the popping of
the bursting seed pods, and discovered that she was
sitting on an ants' nest, the midday bells were ringing
in the white town below her, and it was time to
crawl down the hill again to *déjeuner*.

With *déjeuner* the day, as far as literary endeavour
went, fell in ruins for Katharine. With Mrs. Masterman, on the contrary, it dawned. Not indeed for
literary endeavour ; that she regarded as a creditable
délassement for idle spinsters, or, if taken really
seriously, as a somewhat shady occupation in which
mythical, obscure and eccentric people sometimes
make millions, sometimes starved picturesquely.
" Not that Ulick Adare is obscure or mad," she
hastened to say. " At least I hope not, as he's my
cousin. But you know his grandmother, old Lady
Kilbrogan—not the one on my side—used to do
extraordinary things ; take off her shoes and stockings
in church—a sort of Mohammedan idea I suppose.
. . . It was a square pew with curtains round it, I
have always understood. But still most people
might think it—unconventional, shall we say ? "

Katharine said, not without offence, that she might
say it if she liked, and went on to ask if Mrs. Masterman meant to imply that people who wanted to write
had to take their choice between being outsiders or
maniacs. Mrs. Masterman replied that in her limited
experience they were generally one or the other, and
often both, and forthwith transferred her attention
to her neighbour on her right hand.

Mrs. Masterman and Miss Rowan were staying at
a small, dowdy, and confidential hotel that had been,
as it were, in the Masterman family for generations.
Among other out-worn creeds it held to the custom
of the long table, and to the companion belief that
English people enjoy being herded together like
lepers, and segregated from among all other nations.
The visitor, once set in his place at the table, is bound

to his neighbours by a link indissoluble as that of matrimony; nothing save death or departure can bring release from two daily hours of small talk. Conscientious persons go through with it, and endure a brain exhaustion for which no one gives them credit; only those possessed of the great gift of being silent, contentedly, often pitilessly, silent, come out of it unscathed. Every one with whom we talk is either our host or our guest, and by virtue, perhaps, of her strain of Irish blood, the soul of the hostess was in Katharine. As it happened, she had hitherto been privileged to possess that soul in peace. The individual on her left had no desire to be either guest or host; she was one of a tribe of female botanists, who, in virtue of their calling, were habitually late for meals, arriving well on in the menu, hot, hungry, and absorbed in triumphs or failures too momentous for the appreciation of an outsider. On this day, however, their places were vacant; with the almost awful completeness that is the tragedy of hotel acquaintances, the botanical party had gone under with all hands, and the waters had closed over them (a catastrophe not without its advantages where botanical hands are concerned).

Madame of the Hotel had placed a new-comer beside Miss Rowan. A pretty, dark-haired little lady, with lustrous brown eyes, whose general effect suggested that Madame had for once permitted a foreign lamb to stray into the English fold. Katharine was mentally balancing the rival claims of Italy and South America when she overheard the new-comer confide to Madame a request for white wine, in French that faltered in the English mode. Yet not quite English.

The stranger embarked upon the white wine; delicately and with the neatness of a little bird she dipped her small and aquiline beak into the glass. There was a moment of concentrated stillness, her face grew suddenly scarlet, and the inner soul, that does not wait for introductions, looked forth from her brown eyes in horrified appeal to Miss Rowan. After an instant of palpable indecision the mouthful went down.

"Oh, Heavenly Powers!" she gasped, and the South of Ireland lay bare, "that's awful! That's the ugly wine! For gracious' sake, is it poison?"

The all-watchful Madame was already at her elbow, and snatching up the bottle applied her nose to it. "Mais c'est du vinaigre!" she trumpeted to the room at large.

A gale of laughter went down the long tables; it drove the waiters before it from the room; the kitchen, on the farther side of the courtyard, was audibly felled as one man by the jest.

It was the touch of ill-nature that made the whole hotel kin, and in Katharine's subsequent and not uneventful dealings with Mrs. Delanty she did not forget to enter it to her on the credit side that she laughed at her own discomfiture as wildly as the youngest waiter of them all.

That evening Mrs. Masterman and Miss Rowan went as usual to the "Cercle," strolling pleasantly down in the warm dusk, past the scented gardens, and through the spotless streets, and across the Place, pictorial and unreal as a set piece in a theatre, to the pale palace among the horse-chestnuts, with its wide steps, and crimson carpets, and necklaces and diadems of softened lights. They sat in a corridor, waiting for the music to begin, and watched the world and its wives go past. More especially its wives, in garments and hats never intended to see the light of day, dedicated exclusively to *demi-toilette* and the white blaze of electricity. Irridescent beings, clad like fish in shining scales, wafting strange perfumes, twinkling with diamonds, alternated with British dowdiness, dressed in its best, and nerving itself to meet Continental vice with a pathetic confidence in its Sunday gown. The British male came better out of the contest, perhaps for lack of imagination, perhaps for want of ambition. Miss Rowan decided that timidity was at the root of the matter, and said so to Mr. Adare, who had crawled in from his hotel and fallen limply into a chair beside her. " They shelter behind their tailor," she said, " in fact no one gives sufficient credit to the English tailor for his share in creating national character."

" That's very clever," said Ulick Adare, wan and fractious from heat, " but it's my *jour de repos*, and my doctor doesn't allow me to argue."

" Coward ! " said Mrs. Masterman, allowing her blue eyes to rest upon him for a moment, with a charming blend of mockery and caress. " Don't take it lying down ! "

" If you'll let me lie down I'll take anything," replied Ulick Adare, mopping his sallow brow.

" Men are the slaves of convention," pursued Katharine, driving ahead as was her wont, and laying about her in a way that any properly brought up young woman would recognize as thoroughly impolitic. " And the slaves of fashion too ! Their ideal is conformity, and their want of imagination . . ."

" What about your much-admired hunting-kit ? " interrupted Ulick, with the languid contentiousness of a wasp on a wet day. " I should have thought it was the apotheosis of conformity."

" It's the only picturesque dress men have left themselves, and they do well to be rigid about preserving it," retorted Katharine, shifting her ground. " Look at your ordinary country clothes ! Made of grey mud, or yellow mud . . ."

" Children ! Children ! " reproved Mrs. Masterman.

" I'm very ill," said Ulick Adare, " I want to have the last word."

" In my experience the last word is generally ' Damn ! ' " said Mrs. Masterman, serenely, " and this is not the place for it—and there's the bell——"

The electric bell had begun to utter its piercing

summons. Katharine rose, with the light of battle
still in her eye, and flinging, with a warlike gesture,
something frivolous and pale blue about her straight
shoulders, swept into the concert-room in front of her
friends. She was tall and fair-haired ; she walked
easily, in the English manner, with the balance that
is given by out-door games of skill and speed.

" ' The imperial votaress passed on,' " said Ulick
Adare, with an amused tired eye upon her, as she
parted the ranks of the smoothly-gliding foreign
ladies. " I hope she won't knock two or three of
them down en route ! "

They here were enveloped in the attentions of a
menial in gold lace, long black whiskers, and white
calves, who found obvious chairs, and provided unnecessary foot-stools, knowing to a nicety the pusil-
lanimous heart of the English, and the methods, firm
yet courtly, by which the largesse is extracted. The
long concert-room filled apace. Presently, among
the rustling, scented crowd, Katharine espied a group
of the old ladies who gave to her hotel its special
cachet, and among them the incongruous little figure
of her table companion, Mrs. Delanty. Among their
good grey polls her head, with its dark and intricate
achievement of coiffure, and its over-fashionable hat,
was as poignant as a cry for help. " She certainly
has a very neat profile," said Miss Rowan, reverting
to a previous discussion.

" Yes," said Mrs. Masterman, " but it does not
alter my opinion in the least. Good features are
no criterion in Ireland. When William and I were
soldiering over there I knew her type by the hundred.
Very agreeable they are too, when they forget to be
grand. For my part I infinitely prefer them to the
English equivalent."

" Well, I found her most agreeable," said Katharine
still argumentative, " she talked about horses and
hunting all through dinner."

" I believe it is a topic that lends itself to great

breadth of treatment," murmured Ulick Adare spite-
fully.

" You shall both have your collars and chains on
the next time I take you out," said Mrs. Masterman.

The music began. The orchestra crashed into a
concert overture of enormous vigour, and the listeners
leaned back in their chairs and withdrew into that
inner fastness wherein each soul, after its own fashion,
meets the spirit of music. Or bars it out, as the
case may be. Katharine thought that on this sultry
night the spirit of music had rather over-inspired
the brass, which flared and blazed till she felt as if
the walls of her particular fastness were red hot.
She glanced at Mrs. Delanty and her comrades. The
grey polls were making praiseworthy attempts to
nod in time to the music, but were badly hampered
by the fact that the orchestra was dealing with a
movement in seven time. Mrs. Delanty was yawning furtively into her fan ; this, obviously, was not
what she had come to Aix for.

" I feel sorry for her," said Katharine, as, at the
end of the first part, they moved with the slow
crowd towards the card-rooms, and saw Mrs. Delanty
driving her rheumatic team in the same direction.
" She told me she had come here for fun, and was
supposed to be taking care of one of those old ladies
and that she couldn't call her soul her own."

" I should think she could do without one very
well," said Ulick Adare, " especially here. Why
must we talk about her ? She's quite uninteresting.
Here are real old-fashioned sinners to look at. The
sort of people who stab one another in evening dress
in sixpenny magazines."

The green tables stood like islands under the great
constellations of electric light, and round them sat,
and over them leaned, the people of Æsop's Fables,
the conventional vultures and snakes, wolves and
rabbits, pigs and toads, who have been wrested from

their own sphere of innocence to typify human
iniquity.

Katharine slowly insinuated herself into the crowd
that fringed one of the tables ; she peered between
fat necks and bald heads, and watched the conjuring
tricks of the croupiers, and the elaborate tranquillity
of the players. A Japanese officer was among them ;
he did not need to assume that deadly indifference,
he remained his ordinary self, watching the game
with Eastern eyes that took all and gave nothing.

" I declare I'd rather the Jap than any of them ! "
said the entirely Western voice of Mrs. Delanty at
Katharine's elbow, " but you'd be more afraid of
him ! He's like a little idol that a gentleman gave
me one time. Oh, a horrid thing. I lamed two
horses the week I got it ! "

" Have you got it still ? " inquired Mrs. Masterman eagerly, as befitted an amateur of the
occult.

" Indeed, then, I have not ! " replied Mrs. Delanty.
" I gave it to an old nurse of mine and told her it
was St. Patrick !—and it as black as soot ! "

" And what happened ? " said Mrs. Masterman,
with a gleaming eye.

" Nothing at all ! She got the old age pension,
and she only sixty-eight, and she said it was thanks
to Saint Patrick ! "

This singular result of the blending of two faiths
left Mrs. Masterman incapable of response, a position
to which she was quite unaccustomed.

During the days that remained of Miss Rowan's
time at Aix with her friend, Mrs. Delanty became,
as it were, their little dog. She came when they
called, and often when they did not call. She re-
duced the wardership of her old lady to a system
that dovetailed remarkably with the leisure of her
new acquaintances ; she cultivated them with a
success that she owed partly to her accent, partly
to her Irish perceptiveness, and partly to the assistance

of an unexpected and powerful ally, known to
Chaucer as Dan Russel the Fox.

He was, as it appeared, a very particular friend
of Mrs. Delanty, and of him and of his life, both
public and private, she discoursed untiringly to the
respectfully enthusiastic Miss Rowan. She told of
hounds and of puppy-walking, of hunting, and of
horses, young and old, and of the manner in which
she dealt with all these things. She listened kindly
to the fact that Katharine's experience of hunting
consisted of a blank day in Kent on a hireling, and
a frosty one in Cheshire on a carriage-horse.

"A friend of mine told me that all you want in
Cheshire is a donkey and a boat," she said magnificently; "if you could see the stone-faced banks
in *our* country! It's not an old carriage-horse that'd
get you over *them!* I have a young fellow, a four-
year-old, I broke him myself; he'd carry you flying
in any country! But I'll say this for Gus Fitz-
Symons's hounds, if a horse can live with *them* he
can go anywhere!"

To Mrs. Masterman she talked briefly but mov-
ingly, of her widowed state, of her delicate chest, of
the charms of the climate in the South of Ireland,
of her loneliness . . .

"She tells me she wants to take Indian children,"
said Mrs. Masterman, who possessed two of her own,
for whose sake she had deserted William in the East.
"It might not be such a bad idea——"

It was on the steamer, going over to Haute Combe,
on the farther side of Lac Bourget, that Mrs. Delanty
first let fall the intelligence that she had a little
house to let. She, Mrs. Masterman, Miss Rowan,
and Mr. Adare were seated in the usual unsociable
row, on the gridiron benches peculiar to a pleasure-
steamer. The awning was too high to keep out the
sun; the peacock-blue water was too far away to
be companionable, the fellow-passengers were all too
near; the gross and inveterate vapours of hot oil

came and went fitfully, and at intervals a dark and
greasy being sidled from the cabin and polished the
brasses with a rag of Cimmerian blackness. Through
a streaming veil of smoke the white villas of Aix
wavered among the trees, with the grey wall of
Mont Revard towering behind ; the vines down by
the lake-side flaunted their September splendours,
forecasting their own future in every shade of wine
colour, and deep in the green-blue water lay the pine
woods and crags of the Dent du Chat.

"We are an outrage," said Ulick Adare, as the
steamer trampled her way through the reflections,
"a steamer should always be hull down over an
Atlantic horizon. Here is this brute rooting up the
beauty like a pig in a flower garden."

"Oh, Mr. Adare, how *do* you think of the things
you say ? " cried Mrs. Delanty, admiringly, implant-
ing, in her desire to be appreciative, the question
most calculated to humiliate.

"I suppose these poetic similes come naturally to
Irishmen," said Katharine, regarding Mr. Adare with
a steadfast and expressionless eye.

"Well, indeed, there's a thing I've often heard
said in Ireland about some one that was in a passion," continued Mrs. Delanty, expansively, "'the
pigs are out, and running through the potato garden ! '
Many's the time I said it when I rode up to the
meet, and saw the black face Gus Fitz-Symons had
on him ! It makes me think of the hounds when I
look at these little houses down by the water," she
went on sentimentally, regarding a structure that
might have been the progeny of a mosque and a
mediæval castle, " though on earth what they want
with those cupolas all over them I don't know !
The most they'd do would be to hold your Sunday
hat ! Ah ! Miss Rowan, if you could see a meet
of hounds there by the lake-side ! With the red
coats and all ! And I have a little duck of a covert
that holds a fox as neat as a cat in a basket ! 'Tis

B

a perfect little hunting box! I had tenants there the past two years and they doted on the place!"

"How many bedrooms are there?" said Jean Masterman, meditatively.

CHAPTER II

NOTHING but the fact that Mrs. Masterman's cook had a brother buried in Galway would have induced her, she said, to go to Ireland; the rest of the household submitted to exile, not to say social degradation, "in compliment to Cook and Mrs. Masterman." Without this co-operation it is at least doubtful that Katharine would have carried her point.

It was on an afternoon in late October that the emigrants set forth; a cold, yellow, London afternoon, with more than a touch of frost. Behind them in the van travelled a new habit and a new saddle, dedicated to the ideal hunter that the widow Delanty had pledged herself to provide for Katharine; in an adjacent carriage sat Mrs. Masterman's three servants and wept abundantly, in spite of the alleviating circumstance in connection with the cook's brother. Untouched by care, Mrs. Masterman's two little boys sat in the windows of her carriage and played with her Pomeranian puppy, all three alike serenely irresponsible as hand parcels, regarding a journey as an Elysium of penny toys and chocolate; their time for weeping was not yet.

"Are we fools?" said Mrs. Masterman, addressing Ulick Adare from the carriage window, with an eye wild with crowding memories of "old forgotten things," and the forebodings proper to the leader of an expedition.

" One shouldn't trust to appearances," said Mr. Adare, reassuringly, " I'll write to you about it.

" I thought you were coming over to see," said Katharine, over Mrs. Masterman's shoulder, as the train moved off.

Irish voices were in the corridor of the train, casual, comfortable, philosophic. Irish luggage, scarred by many cross-channel transits, encumbered the carriages. As the Irish Sea drew nearer, forth from among the Amalekites came the Irish people, and at every station were drawn, as by a magnet, into the Irish Mail. The night was full of their sociable voices. Katharine thrilled at the sound and added fresh attributes to the ideal hunter that awaited her on the further side of the channel. On board the boat an Irish stewardess prophesied smooth things of the weather, and was ustified. The ode that is their due has not yet been written of steward-esses, and especially of Irish stewardesses. Daily seeing human nature at its most self-centred, morose, and abject, they maintain, with hearts unwithered, their interest, their geniality, and their enthusiasm for conversation, and with each voyage increase their vast acquaintanceship with the family histories of their country. Somewhere in the electric light of an October dawn the dreary stir of cross-channel steamer life began. The clatter of crockery, the voices of male passengers, the ensuing pop of soda water corks, the stealing odour of fried bacon, and through all the voice of the stewardess, cheerful as ever after her night's vigil, going her rounds with cups of tea and conversation.

" Now, Mrs. Grogan, ma'am, we ll be in in half an hour l Will I get you some nice hot water to wash your hands ? "

Through the thin partition Mrs. Grogan's answer came quaveringly to Katharine.

" Ah, thank ye, no. I'll not mind. I'm going to relations."

Here was Ireland indeed! exulted the all-attentive
Katharine. What reliance on the good sense of her
own family! What confidence in the sympathy of
the stewardess, and with what entire understanding
was the confidence received! Ulick Adare had told
Katharine more than once that it was the excessive
common sense of the Irish people that made them
unconventional. She thought of him now and
allotted the incident its place in the letter she was
going to write to him.

Later on in the day Miss Rowan and Mrs. Masterman agreed that even Mrs. Grogan's unexacting
relations might have drawn the line at their appearance. The fleeting gloss of the steamer toilette had
worn away under the stress of two hours in a slow
train ; they were, in the phrase hallowed by custom,
travel-stained, and there were still seven miles to
drive, and on outside-cars. Protest, even outrage,
was in the respectable countenance of Mrs. Parkington Mrs. Masterman's cook, as she stood in the road
behind the station, expectant of a line of flymen,
and was confronted by the steep and shelterless side
of an outside-car, and was requested by its driver
to " sit up " upon it. The driver wore a black
slouched hat ; he had a fair moustache and blue
eyes that smiled upon Mrs. Parkington with the
ineradicable Irish interest in other people, and more
especially strangers Not thus did London cabmen
regard Mrs. Parkington. She mounted the car. A
woman with a black shawl over her head and a bag
of meal on her back deferred her private concerns
to gaze reverentially at the proceedings, as at a
miracle play enacted for her sole benefit. She tucked
in the housemaid's rug, and with a rallying eye at
the carman (whom she addressed as " Jimmy "), told
him he had his load now, and let him mind it. The
cars clattered and swung up an outlying street of
the small town of Cloon, with its low slate roofs,
and its succession of greedy dingy public-houses, and

out into the open country. The long grey road was patched with broken stones ; the ragamuffin walls wandered beside it, sometimes half lost in veils of briars ; white cottages, stark and bare, hailed each other across wide intervals of the green country. Back of all was the blueness and the spirituality of a line of mountains. The air was warm with sunshine and sweet with the smells of autumn and of turf smoke. The cavalcade turned up a by-road and jingled pleasantly along the southern base of a line of hills, low but steep ; the sun smote upon their mantle of furze and bracken, and below the road, to the left, a little vagrant lake burned blue among pale reeds—the tremendous blue of bogwater under a clear sky. The road presently dived into a small fir wood—the first trees encountered by the expedition—and turned steeply uphill. As the cars crawled up it, the voice of Mrs. Parkington's charioteer was audible, encouraging her and her fellow Niobes with the information that there was foxes in these hills as plenty as rabbits.

At the top of the hill a narrow entrance gate presented itself.

"This is Lake View for you !" said the leading driver to his fares. "Stoop your heads now ! "

They dived in between low-hanging branches of fuchsia, still tasselled with crimson blossoms, and up a narrow drive, with big hydrangea bushes on either side pushing blue and pink blooms into their faces. Then the house, small, pale-yellow, and not unpleasing, with two windows on either side of the hall door, and five overhead. A rusty kitchen-range lay on its face upon the grass in front, as if in despair ; several bicycles were propped against each other and the shrubs. Mrs. Masterman and Miss Rowan descended stiffly from their car and advanced cautiously through the open door into the hall. There were voices in the house, and footsteps.

"'Child Rowland to the dark tower came,'"

whispered Katharine. " I'm rather frightened. I
believe it's the wrong house ! "

" I have Katharine's room finished now ! " a
female voice cried jovially from the top of the stairs.
" I hope she'll say a prayer for me in it ! Have you
the teacups unpacked, girls ? I'm dead for want
of tea ! "

" Well, you'll have time to be buried before John
Michael makes the fire burn ! " screamed another
voice, seemingly from the kitchen, the voice of Mrs.
Delanty, emancipated from the trammels of society.
" Come on down, Eily ! "

Mrs. Delanty's tenants retreated precipitately to
the hall door and rang the bell.

" Ah, what good is John Michael ! I'll . . ." the
voice died away, as when the wind goes suddenly
out of a harmonium, and there was a rustling rush
overhead. The bell completed its summons.

" Eily ! Eily ! " hissed the voice, " they've come !
The people have come ! "

" What a fool I am ! " returned Mrs. Delanty in
high sarcasm. " Sure, they haven't left Cork yet !
It's the boy with the cosy corner. Open the door
for him, John Michael ! "

A door opened and a young man took two strides
into the hall, and stood paralysed. His eyes met
those of Mrs. Masterman in dumb, defenceless agony.

" I'm afraid we have arrived earlier than we were
expected," said Mrs. Masterman, apologetically.

The young man, still in agony, murmured something unintelligible ; there was a confused scurry in
the kitchen, a chair fell down, and Mrs. Delanty
came gallantly into action, palpably pulling herself
together. Her head was tied up in a brilliantly
coloured handkerchief that immediately recalled to
Katharine the market at Aix ; her voice, as she
welcomed the newcomers, had recovered the accent
that it had worn there.

She had had friends to lunch ; they had come

over to see the little house ; they had been trying
whether the new range would burn ; and this was
Mr. Fitz-Symons, who had happened to come over
about earth-stopping. Mrs. Delanty, still explanatory, herded her tenants into the drawing-room,
from the window of which Miss Rowan presently
viewed, not without sympathy, the flight, upon
bicycles, of three unknown young women (one of
whom she was to remember in her prayers). A
moment later, and with even deeper compassion, she
caught sight of Mr. John Michael Fitz-Symons, flee-
ing as a bird unto the hill ; perhaps to inspect the
earths, possibly to take refuge in one of them.

CHAPTER III

"TOM COYNE saw him going in off the road
    over a stone gap yesterday, on that roan
horse of O'Callaghan's," said Mr. Augustus Fitz-
Symons, to his step-brother John Michael, as he
stood commandingly on an island among the puddles
in his stable-yard. "He's a swaggering young pup,
by all I can hear !"

John Michael, who was thoughtfully painting with
Condy's fluid a white patch on the knee of a chestnut mare, paused and looked up.

"Ye'd put four children between himself and the
saddle," said Tom Coyne, with precision and simplicity, while he swiftly applied a water-brush to the
mane of his master's elephantine brown horse.

"That roan's a big-jumped horse," said John
Michael, repulsing without resentment the muddy
blandishments of a broken-haired fox-terrier, "we
might see some sport if he's on him to-day."

"If you'd attend to your own business, that'd be

sport enough for you," said Mr. Fitz-Symons, loosing
his thong venomously at Dhoosh the terrier. " Look
at your boots the way they are after that dirty brute !
Hurry on now and have done with that nonsense !
Do you think there's one in the country doesn't
know her knees are broken ? "

The master pushed his stirrup on to his toe, and
with an effort swung his long thick leg over the back
of the brown elephant.

" Don't you hear what I'm saying to you ? Get
away down and get the hounds out, and hurry on
you too, Tom Coyne ! Don't forget to tell Bridget
she'll get the sack if she lets that harness-room fire
out again ! There isn't one of you's worth a curse ! "

Tom Coyne darted like a rabbit into an adjoining
stable and burst from it again on his horse's back,
with little more than an inch between his spine and
the top of the doorway, according to the precarious
practice of his class.

Hunting mornings broke stormily, and with anything but their conventional joviality, in Mr. Fitz-
Symons's establishment, and it was well understood
that the mood of the master was not one to be trifled
with. His step-mother knew it and did not fail to
leave the whisky on the sideboard ; it gave tone to
the stomach, she said. John Michael knew it, and
was wont at breakfast time to inquire tactfully after
the injured riding-muscle that gave such moral
support to Mr. Fitz-Symons on days when the fences
looked big. Tom Coyne knew it too, but beyond
shortening by a link or two the brown horse's curb
chain on frosty mornings he took no special precau-
tions. There was one thing that Tom Coyne would
not do for his master, or any one else, and that was
to shorten the brown horse's oats.

This morning was not frosty ; it was rough and
soft, as became the south-west of Ireland, and Sam,
the brown horse, proceeded with becoming gravity
along the wet grey road, paying no more attention

to the ever-shifting hounds that surrounded him than
an ironclad does to a school of porpoises. John
Michael, the Whip, and Tom Coyne, general utility
man, jogged astern, incessantly and unconsciously
studying the hounds and exchanging confidences
about them, and, indeed, anything else that occurred
to them, on terms of perfect equality. John Michael's
velvet cap had greenish high-lights ; the skirts of his
scarlet coat were stained, as if with black currant jam,
by the mud of many a boggy ditch, and the toe of
one of his boots had been bitten by a fox in a way that
defied mending ; in fact, Mr. Fitz-Symons had said
that the devil might mend it, and the matter had
ended there.

John Michael was a younger brother of the old-
fashioned tribal type, who existed happily, and penni-
lessly, under the suzerainty of his elder brother.
There had, indeed, been a vague period when he was
" going to be a doctor," during which he had acquired
by some process of natural selection such facts as were
of value to him when he relapsed into the state to
which he was born, kennel-boy, stable-helper, and his
mother's right-hand man. His dark good-looks
suggested some vagrant strain of the Spanish blood
that has touched the western coast-people of Ireland,
and warmed them like the Gulf-stream ; his greatly-
admiring mother had many times asserted that if
'Gustus would only give Johnny the money to go to
England, some rich lady would treat herself to him.

Nothing, it may be said, was farther from the aspirations of John Michael than the career of a professional beauty. The process of earning a livelihood
presented itself to him in but one form, that of picking
up a " likely colt," and " passing him on." What
remained of his mental horizon was occupied by the
hounds ; and, after all, there are many horizons less
desirably filled.

The footing of Mr. Fitz-Symons's Hunt, as a Hunt,
is not easily defined. It had once been a " Sunday

Pack " of harriers ; it had spent a summer as otter
hounds ; and, having had a relapse into hare-hunting
this time on a conventional week-day basis, it had
remained for Mr. Augustus Fitz-Symons to lead it as
a bride to the altar, and there to bestow upon it his
own Mastership, and the title of Mr. Fitz-Symons's
Foxhounds. Their entry into legitimate drama was
regarded with unassuageable suspicion and contempt
by the lawful three-days-a-week county pack, the
X.H., on whose outskirts they lay. The position of
the X.H. was the well recognised one of not wishing
to draw the disputed country themselves, and of
strenuously combating the right of any one else to
do so. But Mr. Fitz-Symons had not for nothing
started in life as a solicitor ; he had written letters
that had commanded the reluctant respect of the X.H.
committee, and (which was more to the point) had
thereby brought about what the sporting papers
called " an amicable arrangement." This meant that
Mr. Fitz-Symons carried his point, and that the X.H.
reserved to themselves the privilege of being aggrieved
for all time and of planting out their best and most
blistering hunting-stories upon the upstarts. It also
meant that when a visitor from the X.H. came over
the border, he found himself going as he seldom went
in his own country ; while the young bloods of the
Fitz-Symons' regime, filled with jealousy as with new
wine, mobbed him as small birds mob a rock, and, as
such a one, limping home embittered, is reported to
have said, " they belted the family coach-horses to
that degree that not one of their mothers could drive
to her prayers the next Sunday."

When Mr. Fitz-Symons rode at the head of his
sixteen and a half couples into the village of Kyleroe,
he was immediately and pleasurably aware of the
presence of two beautifully attired strangers, a young
lady and a young gentleman, among the dozen or so
of riders that awaited him there. This moment of
arrival at the meet was the one that compensated Mr.

Fitz-Symons for many that went before it, even for
many that came after. It was then that he skimmed
the cream of his position and enjoyed the maximum
of pictorial effect with the minimum of danger. He
took off his cap with a largeness that displayed not
only the geniality of the typical M.F.H., but also the
fact that at eight-and-forty his sleek black hair had
little cause to fear the daylight. His importance, his
long and imposing nose, the sacerdotal dignity of his
smile, would have become a Bishop at a Church
Congress.

His flock, it must be admitted, were less decorative.
It was but disjointedly, and in spots, that they conformed to the usual standards of costume in the hunt-
ing-field, and the excessively fashionable pink coat
of the strange young gentleman had as advantageous
a background as even its owner could have desired.
Of the local contingent every member understood
minutely what each of his fellows might or might not
do at any given juncture ; even better each knew
what the horses of his fellows were good for. The
sight of an unknown young lady, arriving with Mrs.
Delanty, on Mrs. Delanty's Dermot—and it was
immediately noted that Dermot and the young lady
were not enjoying one another's society—was sufficiently stirring, but the arrival of the young gentleman on the long-tailed chestnut (grudgingly assessed
by every man present at three figures) was a much
more serious affair.

"That's a great dandy ! " Mr. Clery, the mill-
owner, murmured to young Doyle. "Is he any
good ? "

"How would I know ! " said young Doyle, eyeing
the stranger with the resentment proper to the occasion. "He's by the way of learning farming down
at X——. I believe he failed for the Army. They
say he's full of money. There was a fellow from that
side told me he'd ride a sparra across a country ! He
mightn't do it here ! "

" Well, that flash chestnut he's riding has no more body on him than a crow ! " rejoined Mr. Clery, and felt something comforted.

Both gentlemen here became absorbed in the spectacle of the presentation to the Master of Mrs. Delanty's lady friend.

" I'm told she has £800 a year," said young Doyle, reverentially. He himself had £80, and kept a horse on it.

" She's a stylish looking girl," said Mr. Clery, eyeing Katharine with much-enhanced interest. " She could do without it better than some."

" Did ye hear she gave the widow seventy-five sovereigns for that brown horse of hers ? " said Mr. Doyle.

" God help her ! " said Mr. Clery.

" I'm not saying it's not paying for every hair in his tail," said young Doyle, " but if there was any one would ride him out, he's a good little horse."

A sun that was like a polished pewter plate looked out through trailing scarves of mist as the hounds moved off to draw Knockcarron Wood. At the master's stirrup ran Andy Norris, poacher, shoemaker, and earth-stopper, proclaiming his achievements with chapter and verse.

"Two and twenty big holes I had closed before it was making day, let alone the badgers' dins that I shut last night ! Look ! I put a nick in the stick for every hole of them ! "

He held up a notched hazel rod.

" If you'd shut your mouth I'd be as well pleased," replied Mr. Fitz-Symons, descending abruptly from the plane of the Church Congress.

Crushing against this horse's heels, the hounds pattered meekly in the mud, discreetly ignoring the curs that shrieked and yapped at them from the cottage doorways, ever mindful of the detonating thongs of John Michael and Tom Coyne. The Field jogged behind them, that jog behind hounds, which, coming at the beginning of the day, is frequently a more strenuous affair for the rider than the word would suggest. Mrs. Delanty's friend, on Mrs. Delanty's brown horse, was sitting her tightest (which was not very tight), and holding her hardest; a loop of pale hair had already detached itself from the heavy plaits at the back of her head, and the colour had mounted to the brim of her hat, which was not as straight as it might have been. Mrs. Delanty's eye, as she watched her disciple, was not devoid of anxiety.

The "flash chestnut" with his back up and his neck arched to iron, was showing off generously; his rider, with a cigarette wedged in the corner of his mouth, strove, not ineffectually, to sustain that expression of wearied calm that has been created and perfected by the motor man. He was a lengthy youth, with a large nose, and he wore his hat slightly on the back of his head; a close observer—in other words, Mr. Clery—could perceive an occasional nibble with the spurs when the enthusiasm of the chestnut showed symptoms of waning.

"It's well to be young!" thought Mr. Clery, indulgently.

Jimmy Doyle said to himself: "That's a quality horse, but wait till we see him coming down the south side of Skeagh!"

"Crammer's pup!" summarized old Captain Bolger, who had been in the Militia.

The road ran between hills, brown and abrupt on one hand, low and green on the other. Between the road and the wood glided in full flight the little Carron river, hung over by the trees whose roots it had undermined; sometimes quiet and dimpling and deep, sometimes falling into sudden and passionate combat with brown-backed boulders; purposeful, self-engrossed, darkly romantic, and by no means an agreeable little river to deal with for those who wish to leave Knockcarron Wood in a hurry when hounds are slipping away outside it. Half a mile from the village the boundary wall of Knockcarron Wood was reached and the Master drew rein. The shoemaker darted forward, lifted an old iron gate off its hinges, and flung it inside the wall; the hounds pressed after him and burst into the wood, headed by Dhoosh the terrier, leaving their master in the act of uncovering his head, and thus depriving him of another of his best moments, that of gracefully capping hounds into covert. Mr. Fitz-Symons was, however, a man of resource. He turned to Miss Rowan, whose mount had not relaxed his efforts till he had established himself at the Master's elbow.

"That's the way I like to see hounds go into covert, Miss Rowan! Ready to eat it! John Michael!" he continued, "go on through the wood with them! Let you watch the back of the covert, Tom Coyne; and Andy Norris, away with you and knock that gap at the western end for us."

These orders having been issued with Wellingtonian severity and obeyed in respectful silence, Mr. Fitz-Symons, still in the grand manner, placed himself across the gateway, and faced the Field, like Horatius on the Bridge.

There was a convention that Mr. Fitz-Symons was his own Huntsman. Mrs. Delanty, talking to Captain Bolger a few yards away, heard the Master, as she had so often heard him before, instructing the newcomer in the tragic history of the riding-muscle, how it interfered with the handling of his hounds in the thick coverts, "where a Huntsman had more walking to do than a man that would be beating for cock," how he had trained his step-brother, who was an active fellow—though not as active as he had been himself —to take them through the coverts for him; and how owing to his—Mr. Fitz-Symons's supreme knowledge of the country and the foxes, he could always " catch a hold " of his hounds, once they got away. This was an attitude in conversation in which Mrs. Delanty was herself an expert, and it seemed to her that the Master's methods lacked subtlety.

" I suppose he's heard she's got money," she said to herself, while she directed at the venerable Bolger a glance that assured him that all her thoughts were his.

Captain Bolger, on his part, while assimilating the glance with enjoyment, said to himself that the stranger must be English, otherwise she would know better than to come to the wrong side of the county, and live cheek by jowl with the little widow. This was ungrateful on the part of Captain Bolger. As a matter of fact, when Mrs. Delanty had come to live in the neighbourhood, he had let her a house, and had simultaneously stated that she reminded him of a French Marquise. Some one else had bettered this by suggesting an Italian countess ; Mr. Fitz-Symons had summarized her as " Continental looking, but a perfect lady " ; and then all similes had been extinguished by the discovery that she was the daughter of a County Limerick butter merchant, and had closed her educational career by running away at the age of seventeen with a Tipperary horse dealer. There came a sudden pause in the enthusiasm for Mrs. Delanty. Nevertheless, the horse dealer being but remotely involved (having broken his neck in a point-to-point, some five years after his marriage) Mrs. Delanty's dark eyes and arching eyebrows reasserted themselves, and after a brief period of indecision, the neighbourhood resumed its acceptance of Mrs. Delanty, with a comfortable sense of condescension, even of compassion.

CHAPTER IV

UNTOUCHED by social cares, John Michael, on Lottery the chestnut mare, slipped away along a mossy ride after his hounds. Upon him was the pressing anxiety of providing sport for the strangers ; in his heart was the knowledge that there had been something far from reassuring about the reassurances of Andy Norris. Knockcarron Wood could usually be trusted to hold a fox, but much depended on the last draw of the Kyleroe Coursing Club, the members of which were as thoroughly friendly and untrust-worthy as their own horde of brindled greyhounds and yellow curs. There was that also about the de-portment of the hounds that led their huntsman to fear the worst. He was now near the centre of the wood, and so far nothing had happened. Three or four couple had come out into the ride, and were wait-ing for him in idleness and frivolity. Patience, low be it breathed, was sitting down and scratching her-self, thoughtfully and luxuriously ; Pilgrim was rol-ling, Charmer was nosing without interest a mossy stone, and Rachel, John Michael's trusted Rachel, was standing in the middle of the ride, aimlessly waving her stern and smiling benignly.

"He's not in it," thought John Michael gloomily ; aloud he said with ferocity—

"What are you at there, Rachel ! Hanging about ! Ger' away there into covert ! "

Rachel turned upon him an eye of melting love, showed her yellow old teeth in a grin of apology, and whisked into the bracken and briars among the stunted oak trees, accompanied by her fellows and by the vituperations of John Michael. After this came a prolonged silence, broken only by the mellow ad-monitions of John Michael to the unseen hounds, as he slowly traversed the well-known passages of the wood.

"Find him and push him out, m'lads! Hike! try for him there!"

A touch of the horn.

"Try! Try! Try!"

John Michael chanted his morning liturgy in a very dulcet tenor voice; a gabble of feverish yelps from a puppy was the only response. There followed immediately a mighty crackling of withered briars, and a rabbit shot like a bullet across the ride; the puppy, pursuing with ingenuous ardour, was met in mid-chase by John Michael's thong, and the thunders of the Riot Act.

"Confound it all!" said John Michael to himself; while the puppy, who had no more self-respect than the rest of her race, uttered shameless lamentations. "If he was in it at all they should have found him by now! Gustus 'll be fit to be tied."

He knew that there was no question of a fox slipping away unseen; Tom Coyne, and his retinue of Argus-eyed country boys, strung out along the back of the wood, might be trusted for that, and, as he moved down into a shallow glen that divided the wood, he told himself it was a bad chance, but if there was a smell of him in the place at all they'd get it there.

The path was wet and steep, and Lottery picked her way down it as neatly as a dog. She was quite free from the usual pretensions and limitations of her kind. She neither ramped, nor fussed, nor feared; she zigzagged among humps of rock; she crept, braced and tense, on tables of slate over which the spring water ran thinly; when it was advisable to slide, she tucked her tail in and slid; and John Michael gave her her head, or as much of it as was fitting for her to have, and watched his hounds forcing their way down through the undergrowth, with the tips of their sterns reddened by thorns.

c

His questing eyes were gray and green, as if they
had caught up the colours of the rocks and the woods ;
the craft of the woods was in them too, but of other
craft there was none.

There was no fox in all the length and breadth of
the glen, and it was at the end of it, while the hounds
were looking reproachfully at John Michael, and John
Michael was praying that an earthquake might
swallow up the village of Kyleroe with its poachers
and its cur-dogs, that he heard voices ahead of him
in smooth and continuous conversation. He groaned,
recognizing the elaborately refined voice of Mrs.
Delanty.

" Gus has let the lot o' them into the wood ! " he
thought, with the unconquerable enmity that is set
between the Huntsman and the Field. " Well, it
makes no difference now ! "

" . . . Ah, she can't hold poor Dermot," the voice
said indulgently, " he never pulled *me* an ounce after
the first day I rode him. All he wants is to be alone
with the hounds ! We had some of the biggest banks
I ever rode in this country, that day, and he never
put an iron on one of them ! "

" It'd be hard for him ! " thought John Michael,
who remembered Mrs. Delanty's first day out on
Dermot, and the masterly manner in which she had
wrested the lanes to her purpose.

He emerged into the ride.

" Oh, there you are, Mr. Johnny," said Mrs.
Delanty gaily, " what good are you that you haven't
a fox for us ? You don't know Mr. Fanshawe ? This
is our huntsman, Mr. Fanshawe, but he's called the
Whip ! You mustn't make any mistake about that
when you're talking to his big brother ! "

Mr. Fanshawe (summarized by Captain Bolger as
a Crammer's Pup) bore up as best he might against
the intricacies of this introduction, and was spared
a reply by the sudden irruption of the Master into the
ride.

" What the devil are ye at here, John Michael ?
There's hounds hunting, back at the western end
of the wood! You must have drawn over
him ! "

Whatever John Michael's private opinions were he
kept them to himself. The chestnut mare swung
round, and went away down the ride with that headlong yet collected speed that is learned in the school
of adversity by the hunt-servant's horse. Behind
her sped the hounds, mystified but hopeful, and behind them pounded the riders, tasting the doubtful
joy of following their leaders at speed in a wood. At
a junction with another ride John Michael pulled up
and listened. What he heard was the ridiculous
voice of Dhoosh, the kennel terrier, squeaking an
octave above the average canary, and the robuster
tones of Why-not, the biggest babbler in the pack,
in hot and eager duet. It did not satisfy John
Michael, but it was enough for the rest of the hounds.
In the pose dear to photographers of hunts they
stood and stared for a moment as one man, the next,
they were gone, also as one man.

John Michael followed them through the trees, and
the Master sat still, with his hand up. There was
a pause, during which Miss Rowan tried to drag her
habit down over her right foot, with a hand stiff and
shaking from the implacable tug of Dermot, then,
from outside the wood, came a shout, distant and
hilarious.

" Be-jove, he's away ! " said Mr. Fitz-Symons,
sticking out his elbows and hustling right-handed
down a narrow path, with his followers squeezing,
bumping, and jostling behind him. A minute or
two took them to a gateway at the edge of the wood,
to something at least that had been a gateway, and
was now a formidable " gap " of loose stones, tufted
with branches of furze.

The Master stopped short, and inquired of the
elements, with a special reference to the lower

regions, why Andy Norris had not pulled down the gap.

No answer being forthcoming, and the pressure from behind increasing, Mr. Fitz-Symons leaned forward and endeavoured with a practised hand to pull down the obstruction with the crook of his crop ; but Sam, the brown horse, knew from experience what it felt like to have big stones falling on his toes, and swung away from the wall with the activity of a polo pony.

The way was clear for the next comer, and Mr. Fanshawe charged the gap, driving his spurs into the chestnut with quite unnecessary zeal, and receiving in return a generous lift as his horse flourished over the topmost furze spike, while the two bucks that followed on landing provided—according to Tom Coyne's standard of measurement—accommodation for an infant school between rider and saddle. After him came Jimmy Doyle on his black mare, inevitable and unobtrusive ; Katharine was next, redfaced, panting, and torn by doubts as to whether it was manners for her to precede the Master, who was engaged in the singular process of beating his horse and simultaneously pulling him backwards into a briarpatch. She looked back to Mrs. Delanty for counsel, and found herself gazing into the expressionless countenance of Mr. Clery. Mrs. Delanty had disappeared.

" Give him his head. He'll jump that right enough," said Mr. Clery.

Miss Rowan obeyed. Dermot pivoted round on his hind legs, cannoned into the Master and Sam in the briar-patch, was somehow or other straightened at the jump again, and, in the critical instant before a second refusal, received a startling reminder from Mr. Clery's thong that caused him to bounce in some disorder over the wall, taking down the greater part of it with his hind legs.

Katharine was not very clear as to what had

happened, but when she recovered herself she found
that she was, at all events, back in the saddle and out
of the wood, and Mr. Fanshawe's red coat was blazing
like a beacon in front of her. She heard Mr. Clery's
voice behind her.

"I'm sure we're all greatly obliged to you! You
softened the gap nicely for us!"

"I'm so sorry! I hope it doesn't matter," gasped
the benefactress, struggling to readjust her reins to
an even length. "I hope the Master doesn't mind
my having gone in front of him."

"He'll forgive you," replied Mr. Clery, in his sen-
tentious, humorous voice.

Katharine galloped on, bewildered, because everything and everybody was so wholly unlike what she
had expected; uncomfortable, because the ground
was heathery and rough, and Dermot was pulling
harder than ever.

Mr. Clery and Jimmy Doyle then passed out of
existence, and she was aware only of the beacon red
coat, pushing on up the lower slope of a steep brown
hill that faced the covert. Of the hounds nothing
was visible, but on the ridge of the hill were figures
shouting and pointing. She found the hill growing
momently steeper, and the beacon began to take it
in zig-zags; there was a howl from the hilltop, and the
figures vanished, leaving the skyline bare and quite
unsuggestive. Mr. Fanshawe, upon this portent,
attempted a frontal attack, by what might have
been a sheep track, seemed suddenly to realize that
he was attempting the impossible, and precipitately
dismounted. Katharine's saddle was slipping back,
and a disquieting view of Dermot's backbone was
being presented to her; Dermot was blown, but retained his determination to follow his leader.

"I say! I think you'd better get off!" called the
leader from above. "You can't get on and you can't
turn. It's a beast of a place!"

Katharine obeyed. That is to say she flung

herself in a heap into a bush of heather, and Dermot, twitching the reins out of her hand, continued with inveterate sociability to struggle upwards. When Miss Rowan arose, not without difficulty, from her couch of heather, Mr. Fanshawe was in the pleasing position of holding two horses, one perched precariously above him, the other seemingly determined on rushing the position from below.

" Can't you catch him if I turn him down to you ? "

It is a bad thing for a man's temper to be thrown out of a hunt, but when it also happens that a woman —so Mr. Fanshawe expressed it to himself—has piled herself up on his back, he does not, as a rule, succeed in disguising his emotions. " I can't stay here much longer ! " Mr. Fanshawe here thrust the emulous Dermot from him and started him downhill again with a thoroughly unfriendly whack. Katharine felt extremely dubious of being able to do what she was desired, but she realized that if Dermot were a live bomb, or a mad bull, the thing must be attempted. Dermot, however, had not for nothing been " r'ared very pettish on lump sugar " (as Mrs. Delanty's stable-boy had complained). He crept cautiously downwards, as became a horse who had spent the first years of his life on the side of a furzy hill, and even stood still and permitted his rider to climb on to a rock, and thence drag herself into the saddle.

" They're in the next parish by now ! " said her much-tried companion, stumbling down the track behind her, in pallid wrath. " Would you kindly let me pass ? "

Mr. Fanshawe felt that the age of chivalry was past, and rightly so. There was a brief moment of collision, a slither, and a scramble, and the chestnut was ahead, avalanching and glissading to the bottom of the hill.

There Mr. Fanshawe pulled up and listened. There was nothing to be heard but the barking of dogs at a distant farm-house, nothing to be seen but the long,

purple-brown expanse of the wood, with a hawk
hanging in the wind above the tree-tops, and between
the hill and the covert a narrow stretch of grass,
dinted with hoof-tracks that bore away to the right.

When it comes to catching hounds by means of
hoof-dints and the barking of cur-dogs, the case is
next door to desperate. Defeated and exasperated,
the two comrades in misfortune followed the hoof-
tracks, and as they galloped, in the dismal fuss of those
who pursue a vanished hunt, each inwardly said that
it was the other's fault.

They had not to endure it long. The space between wood and hill closed in to a narrow passage,
in which the guiding tracks were swallowed in mire.
Mr. Fanshawe dashed into the slough ; Miss Rowan
splashed in after him, and the black mud spattered
cold on her face and made big blots on the red coat
of her leader. Beyond the slough the wood swelled
outwards and the track widened ; the forlorn hope
galloped and, still galloping, found itself swinging
round a corner where the wood receded again and
formed a bay. A pleasant sward lay in the shelter,
and it was here, without any warning, that the matter
ended.

The hounds were there, seated in a decorous group,
and the Field was there too, standing about conver-
sationally and eating sandwiches.

" No hurry ! " said Jimmy Doyle politely, as the
long-tailed chestnut, with his chin on his chest,
banged into the black mare from behind.

" Well, you and Miss Rowan look as if you had been
round the world for sport ! " said Mrs. Delanty to Mr.
Fanshawe, as, closely attended by the devoted Dermot, he tugged his horse to a standstill beside her.
" You've ridden a great finish anyhow ! *We've* had
a hunt, and a kill too ! Haven't we, Mr. Fitz-
Symons ! "

The master made as if he heard not, and moved
away.

"Look at his cross old back!" tittered Mrs. Delanty. "I declare I'm almost afraid to tell you what happened!"

Katharine was not accustomed to feeling like a fool, or to behaving like one, but it appeared that hunting in Irish backwoods was to enlarge her horizon in these respects. She looked round upon these Philistines with their strange voices and their esoteric jokes, for whom she and her fellow alien had been making sport, and even as she did so, and met the parrot eye of old Bolger, with the withheld wink in it, she realized that these were jovial Philistines, with a kindly feeling for a fool.

"Well, you see, there were a couple of young hounds and the kennel terrier," said Mr. Clery, in mild and leisurely narrative, "and they were very anxious for a bit of fun, and what did they meet only the keeper's cat that was rabbiting there too. He came out over the wall here, the poor fellow." Mr. Clery paused, and regarded Katharine's splashed face. "You should ask Mr. Fitz-Symons for the brush."

"What!" broke in Fanshawe, feeling a little better. "D'ye mean to say that's all they've done? Killed a cat?"

"It was a very fine cat," replied Mr. Clery reprovingly.

CHAPTER V

THERE exists in Ireland (and probably elsewhere, though less frankly admitted) a standard of cleanliness which is embodied in the phrase, "if 'twill do, 'twill do." It is a useful working principle, containing a good deal of sound common sense, but it is occasionally broken in upon by spasms of reformation, the revolt, perhaps, of the artistic nature against monotony, the outcome, more frequently, of the simple desire to impress the stranger. The deep, calvinistic heart of the English spring-cleaning is not in it ; it is a freak, not a religious exercise.

On the Monday following the slaughter of the cat, a spasm of reform, of special severity, convulsed the Ashgrove kennels. It was inaugurated by a surprise visit from the master himself. John Michael was away at a fair, selling sheep for his mother, and his elder brother made the almost unheard-of effort of visiting his keneels before breakfast, that is to say, at the liberal hour of 8.30, with a liver just sufficiently touched up by a north-east wind to stimulate the critical faculty. He then found the hounds still immured in their sleeping apartment ; the outer door of the feeding yard had been left open, and in it two donkeys mused, like the gravedigger in *Hamlet*, over the remains of a comrade who had progressed from the boiler to a wheelbarrow, and there awaited further developments. Save for a thin wisp of smoke the abode of the kennel-boy, some fifty yards away, showed no sign of life. Mr. Fitz-Symons advanced upon it ; as he did so the kennel-boy's mother burst forth, and, in the shock of meeting the master, revealed that she was on her way to " let out the dogs into the yard."

Mr. Fitz-Symons's reception of this intelligence need not be set down, but it at once drove the kennel-boy's mother into the higher realms of fancy. She declared that there was not a day in the year that that little boy wouldn't let a yowl out of himself, below in the kennels, at five o'clock in the morning, but, she called Heaven to witness, he had a gumboil inside in his mouth this three days, and he was dead with it ; it would take him six months to eat a biscuit.

" I can tell you what," returned Mr. Fitz-Symons, with bilious ferocity, " if I catch him again neglecting his work this way, I'll knock a yowl out of him that he'll not forget in a hurry ! "

" May the Lord comfort your honour long ! " replied the kennel-boy's mother, who had weathered worse storms than this.

It was during the same morning that Captain Bolger stood at the open door of Ashmount House, and groped in the ivy for the bell handle.

" Well, bad manners to you for a bell, where are you ? " he soliloquized. " Would the gong do as well, I wonder ? "

He advanced into the hall and sounded a challenge ; a voice from an adjoining room replied :

" What a hurry ye're in ! Can't ye leave it on the table."

" Is it myself I'm to leave on the table ? " said Captain Bolger, regarding with composed enjoyment the consternation of the pretty maid-servant who followed the voice.

" Sure I thought it was the bread-boy," she murmured in deep confusion.

" If I was a young man that was coming looking for you, I wouldn't make so much noise about it ! " returned Captain Bolger gallantly, " where's Master Johnny ? "

" He's at the fair, sir—The Mistress ?—" an obvious hesitation. " The Mistress is out."

" Indeed, then I am *not* ! " cried a jocund voice from the farther side of a door, which, on the words, was flung widely open, " I'm below stairs this two hours, salting pork ! "

Mrs. Fitz-Symons came on with swift and heavy tread, and a countenance that radiated heat and hospitality.

" Never mind John Michael, Captain ! Come in and sit down." She led him into the dining-room. " There's a good fire here and there's none in the drawing-room. I never have a fire in the drawing-room unless there's company, and I'm not going to make company of you ! "

Captain Bolger, nothing loth, lowered himself into a roomy armchair in front of the fire, and affected not to observe that Mrs. Fitz-Symons was abstracting a decanter of port and a cake from the sideboard.

" I came over to ask Johnny could he tell me any-thing about a colt that McCarthy Sowny is trying to sell me.   Isn't he a tenant of Gus's ? "

" Indeed then he is ! " said Mrs. Fitz-Symons, " and I wish he was yours !   He was here last week with the same colt, trying would Gus have him in place of his rent—Gus says he had no more bone than a little dog ! "

" Ho, ho ! " said Captain Bolger, taking, as it were unconsciously, a sip of port.   " Better do without him if that's the way ! "

Mrs. Fitz-Symons picked up a half-knitted stock-ing, and, seating herself at the other side of the fire, began to knit in a comfortable and conversational manner.   The fact that she had on her housekeeping apron, and a tweed cap that had been discarded by her younger son, did not disturb her in the least.

" Well, now, never mind about 'Gustus or the colt either," she began.   " What I want to hear about is the new young lady ! "

" Gus is the man to tell you about her ! " said Captain Bolger, applying himself again to his glass of port.

" Gus didn't tell me as much as if she had a face on her !   That was because they had a blank day, and the hounds made a fool of him with a cat ! " replied Gus's step-mother, with tranquil grasp of the position.

" Well and had Johnny nothing to say about her either ? " said Captain Bolger, with the air of a man flying a kite to bring down the lightning.

The lightning came.

" He said she rode twelve stone, and that the widow's brown horse would have a sore back after her to-day !   You'd know all about her after that,

wouldn't you ! " returned Mrs. Fitz-Symons, witheringly. " I'd sooner ask Tom Coyne any day, and I
did too, and he told me she was a fine handsome
young lady, and that she and the other lady had
Lake View taken for the whole winter. That was
something, anyhow !

" Tom's a pretty good judge," said Captain Bolger,
" and did he tell you she has a fine fortune too, and
that's better than looks ! If you want to make a
match for Johnny, you should order out your phaeton
and go and see her for yourself ! " To himself he
said, " She's a cut above poor Johnny, I'm afraid ! "

" Oh never fear I'll see her soon enough ! " replied Mrs. Fitz-Symons. " I'm too old to go calling
on grand English ladies like them ! They wouldn't
be bothered with me ! "

" Cock them up ! " interjected the chivalrous
Captain Bolger.

" I'd be as well pleased without them indeed,"
continued Mrs. Fitz-Symons, with complete sincerity, " but Johnny told me he heard Gus talking
to Mrs. Delanty about coming over to see the kennels
to-morrow and to bring them with her. It's not
Lily Delanty he wants to show the kennels to at this
time of day ! "

" Times are changed ! " said Captain Bolger. " Do
you remember the kennel-coat he got made for
her the first year he had the hounds ? "

" Is it remember it ! " said Mrs. Fitz-Symons with
a laugh that was like the crow of a cock pheasant.
" Don't I wear it every day of my life feeding the
chickens ! "

" I'll tell her that ! " said Captain Bolger.

" You're welcome ! " said Mrs. Fitz-Symons.
" Smoke your pipe now. I know you have it in
your pocket."

Captain Bolger took out his tobacco pouch and
proceeded to fill his pipe. " Well, well," he mused,
" when all's said and done Lily Delanty's a taking

little woman. That young spark we had out hunting
yesterday rode home with her."

" By what I hear of him she's old enough to be
his mother ! "

" Come now, it's not as bad as all that," said
Captain Bolger, applying himself to the calculation
of Mrs. Delanty's age with the zest bestowed by
elderly gentlemen on such a topic. " She's had Lake
View three years, and she was pushing five and
twenty when she came here. I thought she and
Johnny were about the one age." Captain Bolger
rolled his full blue eyes at his hostess over the bowl
of his pipe. " You might remember that the people
were saying that time that they'd make a nice pair ! "

" Little the poor child thought about her ! " exclaimed Mrs. Fitz-Symons, giving the fire an indignant
stab with the poker, " but indeed as for her, the
world knows she paid him every court ! Knitting
ties for him, and giving him silver match-boxes,
and tobacco-pouches, and all sorts of trush ! Didn't
I say to him ' Johnny, my lad, why wouldn't you
ask her for a breeches ' ? "

" Ho, ho, ho ! " roared Captain Bolger, " that was
something practical ! "

" Well, and wasn't it sense for me ? " returned
Mrs. Fitz-Symons, undaunted. " I can tell you
that's the lady that looks both sides of a sixpence !
Didn't they say that when Delanty died she sold
every stitch of the poor man's clothes at the auction !
Boots and breeches and all ! And herself out in the
town cutting eights on her bicycle in front of the
hotel, no more than a fortnight after his death ! "

" Ah well, she mightn't do that for John Michael,"
said Captain Bolger, soothingly.

Mrs. Fitz-Symons eyed him for a moment almost
pityingly.

" She might not indeed," she said, " but if you're
asking me my opinion—and I'm not saying you
are—I don't think she'll get the chance ! "

Mrs. Fitz-Symons was too much of an artist to mar the calm of this statement by any change of expression, but her knitting needles flashed like rapiers.

CHAPTER VI

KATHARINE was an orphan and an only child, circumstances for which pity is conventionally due; yet they are not without their advantages. Having spent a nomadic childhood in expensive schools and the residences of uncles and aunts, rich, for the most part, and affectionate, she was now, at the age of twenty-six, that rare and enviable creature, an independent young woman, enjoying to its ultimate half-crown the income that would have been her eldest brother's had he existed. Her trustees passed on to her, beautifully and inevitably, her dividends; the straps of her trunks bounded her responsibilities; she was free to come and go as she listed. The high gods looked down in disapproval upon an existence so ideal, and decreed that she should take upon herself the care of a horse.

In the dark of the winter dawn, Katharine, lying awake in deep brooding upon saddle-room stoves, heard Dermot cough in his box. Did horses get bronchitis? Had she already broken his wind? She would telegraph for a book on The Horse. Following on the cough came bangs on the stable door; was he calling for help? Caroline, the housemaid, who answered her bell, opined that the poor 'orse wanted his feed, and Caroline was an authority, because her father was a cabman, and her sister had driven in chariot races at Olympia. It was apparent that fair as had been the professions of Mr. Timothy McCarthy, her new retainer, in the matter

of early rising, he had not lived up to them, and his
employer dressed moodily, composing an exordium
that should set forth his duties without revealing
her own ignorance. The exordium was delivered
with a fair show of confidence, but was immediately
countered by the statements that the horse's legs
was all filled up after the night, and that the cook
refused him the key of the coal-house, and that it
was an unnatural kind of a stove that was in the
harness-room. She was also informed that he hadn't
so much as a pike to make up a bed. Miss Rowan
retired, worsted, to meditate upon that power of
placing a blameless employer in the wrong that is so
unsparingly wielded by even the most lenient of
servants. She also determined to ask Jean Masterman if her experience of the cavalry enabled her to
throw any light upon the nature and functions of a
pike.

Katharine went round to the front of the house.
The sun was warm on her face, a delicate warmth,
like the kindness of a sensitive hand. The breeze was
light and westerly, and had dinted the surface of the
lake with little sharp ripples ; between the stems of
the fir trees a flare of sunshine struck up from the
water, flakes and drifts of gold lingered on the branches
of the beeches, the sky was blue, the boggy sweetness was in the air. Ulick Adare, she thought, would
have said it all very well in an article ; one of those
articles of his that frightened her by their perceptiveness, not alone of Nature. She sat down on a
garden seat of " rustic " habit, that partook of the
general meretricious discomfort of the Delanty furniture, and thought a little about Ulick Adare. Life
would be impracticable if men, in addition to their
other advantages, were as perceptive as women ;
happily it was impossible to be frightened by Ulick
Adare ; with all his perception he was, like many of
his countrymen, too agreeable to be feared. If he did
not change his mind at the last moment he was to be

with them next week. His mind, he said, was too well balanced, and tilted responsively to every grain of argument. She idly wondered if it would tilt for a picture post-card, if such were procurable.

"Katharine," said Jean Masterman, from an upper window, "I've just had a note from your friend Delanty. She will call here for us with that youth in his motor at three o'clock, and take us to the Kennels. Excellent little woman! She lost no time in getting her claws into him! She's worth ten of *you*!"

"I wonder you don't realize how monotonous your point of view is!" responded Katharine. "Anyhow, no one can say that I did not run after him yesterday out hunting!"

"You don't know how to run!" said Jean Masterman, and withdrew from the window.

Mrs. Delanty was as good as her word. At three o'clock Mr. Fanshawe's motor uttered its summons at the gate, and Katharine and Mrs. Masterman took their appointed places behind him and the promoter of the expedition. The distance was but five miles, but in these matters time is "counted by heart throbs, not by figures on a dial," and those who drove with Mr. Fanshawe lived every moment, and expected that each would be the last. As Mrs. Masterman and Katharine bounded on their seats, and swung into each other's laps, they thanked heaven that they were not in front, and were, at all events, spared the anticipation of the donkey carts and the children. What Mrs. Delanty felt they could only surmise from her convulsive grasp of the arm of her seat; the rapture of an unceasing succession of "near things" remained with Mr. Fanshawe.

"Under the twelve," he said, pulling off his gloves at the entrance of the Ashgrove Kennels. "We'll make better time going back, down hill." With this exhilarating prospect before them the ladies disembarked.

Mr. Augustus Fitz-Symons was prepared to enjoy himself. He had on a clean kennel-coat, and the white linen flattered his broad shoulders and dark looks; he had had his hair cut and had bought a new cap (points that were reverently appreciated by his brother and the kennel boy). His visitors, moreover, were strangers, and Mr. Fitz-Symons had an instinctive preference for strangers, the preference, perhaps, of the man who has a shop window and not much to put in it. He shook hands with his guests, lingeringly and possessively, the type of handshake that is liable to set in at about the age of forty-five, and indicates that, though appearances are against it, the ardour of youth still informs that which might have been mistaken for merely paternal kindness. In Miss Rowan's case he even retained her hand, while he enquired how she and her horse had felt after their day with the hounds.

"Ah, we'll show you something better than that!" he said, allowing his brown eyes to dwell upon her.

Mr. Fitz-Symons satisfied his own ideals best when he had, as it were, elbow room, and there was no need for hurry. He now was King Solomon, majestically preparing to exhibit his apes and peacocks, and Katharine, quickly apprehending the position, was aware that not Jean Masterman, nor yet Mrs. Delanty, but she herself, had been cast for the rôle of the Queen of Sheba. On her was bestowed the only spare kennel-coat, the Master's own whip was placed in her hand, and she was conducted into the kennel-yard, where, with her back morally as well as actually against the wall, she stood like a general taking the salute, while hound after hound was paraded before her, and the difficulty of composing encomiums became momently greater (a difficulty that, possibly, does not press heavily upon Generals).

Outside the rails, representing merely the general public, was the remainder of the party, was even Mrs.

D

Delanty, the last authority on the hounds, the patentee of the strangers. To expound the pack to Mr.
Fanshawe from beyond the pale, as she was now
doing, was certainly a consolation ; to draw attention
to Rainbow, whom, as a puppy, she had nursed
through distemper, or Cardinal, who through her good
offices had been acquired from a Welsh pack, or
Rosemary, who was so shy she wouldn't let the
Master put a hand on her, though she, Mrs. Delanty,
could do anything with her. Mr. Fanshawe thought
her wonderfully knowledgeable (as indeed she was),
and admired her with the conventional, almost inevitable admiration of a tall fair man for a small and dark
pretty woman ; Mrs. Masterman, who neither knew
nor desired to know anything of the matter in hand,
kept her handkerchief to her nose, and devoted her
attention, as was her wont, to the social aspect.

The person, who, so far, appeared to have no social
aspect or aspirations, was Mr. Fitz-Symons' younger
brother. He had probably not yet recovered from
the shock of his first encounter with the tenants of
Lake View, and having tendered a limp hand for the
acceptance of the ladies, he had faded away into the
kennel, and the performance of his duties as kennel-
man.

Miraculously, as it seemed to Katharine, he extracted hound after hound, as required, from the
throng in the darksome recesses of the kennel ; he
was very quick and quiet in his handling of them, and
the lambent eyes of those who still waited for their
turn glowed upon him with frankest homage. It is
a privilege of dogs, which has not been extended to
human beings, to look their best when they are beg-
ging. The pockets of the Master's kennel-coat
bulged with broken biscuit, and the knowledge of it
penetrated the very souls of the hounds, making them
romantically, passionately, beautifully greedy. Mr.
Fitz-Symons, still with the air of King Solomon dis-
pensing largesse, presented a handful to Miss Rowan,

who was straightway beset by a gang of sturdy beggars, all indisputably, looking their best, and all well aware that this was probably the chance of a lifetime. Katharine was hustled into a corner by them ; one hound snatched at her hand, another pushed a determined snout into her pocket, a third tried, not without success, to lick her face, and it was at this juncture that she found John Michael at her side.

" She was walked by a lady," he murmured in his gentle brogue, while he dealt Dauntless an entirely ungentle clout with his whip.

" How heartless ! " said Katharine, extending a consolatory piece of biscuit. Two hounds jumped at it like sharks, and in the same instant her hand was caught away by John Michael, and held, biscuit and all, while two pairs of jaws clashed like rat traps.

" They'd take the hand off you like that ! " he said, looking at Miss Rowan with gentle reproof, as if she were a child. His hazel eyes were clear and serious, his manner was that of an earnest young Sunday school teacher. " See now," he continued, " you should hold the bit in the palm of your hand, like this." He said " the pa'm o' yer hand," with entire simplicity, there was not a shade of self-consciousness in his grave eyes ; where hounds were concerned John Michael would look any man or woman in the face.

Katharine had not escaped the effeteness of the artistic temperament, if, indeed, it be effete to take a conscious pleasure in simplicity, and she savoured the quality in John Michael with a new and intricate enjoyment.

" Was Miss Rowan frightened by poor Dauntless ? " shrilled Mrs. Delanty, who, during this episode, had been talking to the Master through the rails.

" She was not," replied John Michael, expressionlessly.

" Ger' away back, Hounds ! " thundered the Master. " What are you about, John Michael, letting them knock a lady about, like that! I must apologize, Miss Rowan, for the rudeness of my hounds," he went on, with the manner of treacle and pomp that he reserved for the highest female society, " it is not often they're honoured by visits from strange ladies ! "

" They know fast enough who's afraid of them ! " said Mrs. Delanty to Mr. Fanshawe, on the wrong side of the railings.

" We'll see them fed now," continued Mr. Fitz-Symons, ushering Katharine protectively into the feeding yard. " Where's that boy ? Dinny ! " He strode into the boiler-house, and the kennel boy staggered forth with a bucketful of soup and fell to his task.

Mrs. Masterman buried her face in her muff. Mrs. Delanty poked her stick into a slab of yellow porridge in the feeding-trough, and examined its point critically. Katharine recognized the stick as one that they had bought together at Chambéry, when nothing on earth could have seemed more improbable than the present moment.

" I'm afraid your *chef* is run out of oatmeal, Mr. Fitz-Symons. Johnny, you and I made a better pudding than this that time every one had the ' Flu ! ' There was no talk of skimping the oatmeal then ! "

Mrs. Delanty flung this barbed reminiscence at the Master's broad white back ; it fell, apparently, unheard, but the space of neck between his collar and his black hair deepened in colour.

Mrs. Masterman put up an eyebrow at her young friend over the top of her muff. Was this indeed, it seemed to say, the pliant and subservient Delanty, she who at Aix had been their little dog, a little humble dog, incapable of a snap ?

" Oh, I say, Mrs. Delanty ! " burst in Mr. Fanshawe, who during the proceeding had babbled ceaselessly and facetiously, " how many hounds died of it ? The pudding, I mean, not the ' Flu ! ' "

" One," said the Master, turning viciously round, " he swallowed a hairpin ! "

CHAPTER VII

WELL, I hope you enjoyed that!" said Mrs.
Masterman in Katharne's ear, as they
emerged at length from the feeding yard and its
sights and scents. "If I knew Mrs. Fitz-Symons
well enough I should ask her for brandy!"

Miss Rowan turned her back upon her friend, and
handing her kennel-coat to John Michael, thanked
him for the entertainment with a warmth that seemed
to his elder brother misplaced.

"Here, you can hang this up too," he said, flinging
his own coat at his junior. If Miss Rowan did not
know who was top-dog at these kennels, the sooner
she learnt it the better.

John Michael obeyed the behest with alacrity.

The sun had dropped over the ridge of the long
brown hill that lay behind the kennels, and the yellow
sky was clamorous with rooks, swinging home to the
tall ash-trees that gave Ashgrove its name. Mrs.
Delanty had, as she said, "Stuck to the ship," and
had gone round in the motor with Fanshawe. Mrs.
Masterman and Katharine accepted their host's in-
vitation to walk, and now, in cumbersome motor
coats, were toiling along the short cut across the
fields. The mud lay in sloughs in the gateways, and
formed a holding paste on the paths; Mrs. Masterman walked with Mr. Fitz-Symons, enduring her
sufferings with fortitude, and to John Michael fell
of necessity the task of escorting Miss Rowan.

John Michael's two white terriers, Dhoosh and
Sue, arose from the lair in the straw-rick from which,
with hatred undimmed by repetition, they daily
watched the feeding operations, and fleeted in the
darkening fields like spirits released from purgatory.
John Michael, frowning with shyness, watched them

furtively from under his black brows, and even while
he uttered the monosyllabic replies that were his
contribution to the conversation, he was thinking
that Dhoosh had the legs of Sue, but she could best
him when it came to dodging.

They came to the final gateway near the house ;
the cows had gathered there, awaiting their evening
milking and their admission to the much desired
cowhouse, in motionless expectation that took no
heed of the chilly sea of mud in which they stood.
Mr. Fitz-Symons halted.

"Drive them out of that," he said to his step-
brother.

John Michael advanced upon them with understanding, from the side, calling out "How-how-
haow !" after the manner of Munster, and the cows
slowly began to move, swinging their heads at the
terriers in heavy contempt, as these Jacks-in-office
charged dramatically into the mire, and enforced
their owners' commands with short bullying rushes
and yappings.

"I think we'll have to carry you ladies over this !"
said Mr. Fitz-Symons, regarding his guests with
facetious gallantry.

John Michael began hurriedly to pull heavy stones
out of the wall by the gate, and to arrange them as
stepping-stones ; his faun-like alarm at being involved
in his brother's suggestion could not have been more
frankly indicated. He himself stood in the mud,
with the unconcern of one of the cows, and proffered
an entirely remote and impersonal elbow for the
assistance of the ladies. Jean Masterman, hopping
like an enormous fur-clad bird, from stone to stone,
said to herself that she would remember John Michael
in her will.

Nothing remained for Mr. Fitz-Symons save to
follow in the wake of the ladies.

"You can stay and build up that wall again,"
he said as he passed his brother.

John Michael said nothing, and stayed.

Mrs. Fitz-Symons' drawing-room was a wonderfully perfect relic of the earliest Victorian period. It had the rare merit of being entirely consistent ; nothing save its myriad framed photographs spoke of a more recent date than 1850, and Mrs. Fitz-Symons, in a cap with pink ribbons and a well-matured black silk dress, was agreeably in the picture. There was a mighty fire, every window was shut, and a tall, unshaded lamp held the room in its search-light glare, and exerted a mesmeric spell upon the eyes and the intellect. Mrs. Fitz-Symons was wholly impervious to spells of any kind, and was, moreover, possessed of the enviable Early Victorian constitution, that thrives in the extreme of heat and the minimum of fresh air ; she sat in front of the fire and wielded a genial teapot, whose contours and general expression were not unlike her own, and obviously enjoyed herself. Mrs. Masterman, who had served her time to many hostesses, and was herself no mean exponent of the art, realized almost immediately that here the burden of the guest would lie lightly upon her. There were other guests, two or three unknown young ladies, daughters of the land, who plied with teacups and cakes, and were not worthy, it appeared, of being introduced to the strangers ; the Master of the house dealt forth to each of them a finger and a Christian name, selected a comfortable chair beside Miss Rowan, and permitted their ministrations with the tranquillity of the Grand Turk.

Katharine found herself engaged in a triangular conversation with him and one of the tea-bearers, a young lady with a snub nose of the type that, singularly enough, guarantees its owner as unsnubbable. Mr. Fitz-Symons addressed her as " Eily " ; something in her voice was reminiscent of another scene of activity. Was this that " Eily " who, from the staircase landing of Lake View, had sounded the

alarm, the " Eily " for whom Katharine was to say
a prayer ? There was a wary spark in Eily's eye
that showed that she also remembered.

When two of a neighbourhood are concerned in
conversation with an outsider, it is well for the outsider to advance with caution, with platitude, with
small talk, if, indeed, the great gift of small talk is
bestowed. Pitfalls beset the way, and the predestined
foot of the stranger stumbles over the inadequately
interred hatchet. Thus it was that Katharine, as if by
special inspiration, moved smoothly and conventionally from golf to hockey, to find that Eily's Hockey
Club had an outstanding feud with Mr. Fitz-Symons
in the matter of a playing-field. Conversation became
suddenly acrid, and Katharine imperceptibly withdrew her chair from the danger-zone, and into the
sphere of influence of Mrs. Fitz-Symons. There
all was on velvet ; the discourse was of servants, a
topic that in Ireland is presided over alternately
by the Tragic or the Comic Muse ; a Pipe of Pan,
upon which Mrs. Fitz-Symons, like Pan himself,
could " blow in power."

" . . . Mrs. Delanty found her for me," Mrs.
Masterman was saying. "My cook says she seems
a very obliging girl, but nothing will get her up in
the morning."

"Oh then, well I know them ! " responded Mrs.
Fitz-Symons fervently. " I have one this minute,
a great, good-natured slob of a girl, that'd sit up all
night with you if you were ill, and if you were well,
maybe she wouldn't get out of her bed at all ! "

" Charming as a guest," suggested Mrs. Masterman. " Guests who don't get up are such a help."

"Guests indeed ! " ejaculated Mrs. Fitz-Symons,
gathering in Katharine with her roving blue eye,
well aware that she was making sport for " the
English ladies." " Maybe you'd like another one I
had, that had two of her sisters hid in the house
unknown to me for a month, and she telling me she

didn't know why the cows were going back in their milk, and putting it on the hound puppies that they stole the butter! That one went to America," continued Mrs. Fitz-Symons, now in full possession of the ear of the house, which included two of the attendant young ladies, " and what do you think of her mother ? She was here last week to see me, and ' Ma'am,' says she, ' Ellie's after sending me her likeness from Ameriky, I brought it to show you. Faith I'd hardly know it ! ' says she, ' she got so handsome ! ' ' Show it to me ! ' says I ; and what was it only my young lady had sent a photograph of Queen Alexandra, if you please ! ' Well, indeed, Mrs. Hallahan,' says I, ' her journey throve well with her ! I think I'll be off to America myself ! ' "

The door opened, letting in a shaft of cold air, as if from another and a frozen planet, and Mrs. Delanty and Mr. Fanshawe appeared, followed unobtrusively by John Michael.

" We've been looking at Mr. Johnny's four-year-old," announced Mrs. Delanty, " going round him with candles and wax matches ! Such a time for horse-coping ! But I tell them *I* won't be a party to a deal in the dark ! "

Mrs. Delanty, whose furs were undoubtedly becoming, addressed her speech to the room in general, but her eyes followed John Michael, who had already taken covert behind the upright piano.

" You can't back out of it now, Mrs. Delanty ! It's your show," said Fanshawe, appropriating the speech to himself, with a manner that could not be accused of undue formality. " I told you that I put myself in your hands, you know."

" Well, that's a handful, anyhow ! " returned Mrs. Delanty. " What will you give me out of the bargain, Mr. Johnny ? "

John Michael, who was seated in acute discomfort on a small and creaking music stool, grinned feebly and attempted no rejoinder.

" It's time enough for him to tell you that when
you have it made ! " said his mother, snatching up
the gauntlet.

" Quite right, Mrs. Fitz-Symons ! " said Fanshawe
in his voice of deadly calm. " I understand that in
this country it takes three days and a bottle of—
what d'you call it ?—potteen—to buy a horse ! "

He was a well-meaning youth, yet he had not been
proof against the temptation of over-tranquillity.
Katharine, with a heat generated perhaps as much
by the temperature of the room as by some sub-
conscious championing of the house of Fitz-Symons,
thought his manner a blend of patronage and
asininity.

" Well, indeed, I don't know about that ! " replied
Mrs. Fitz-Symons, eyeing him indulgently. " I
went to an auction here, one time, to buy beds, and
I came back with a mare and foal, and I had the
pair of them bought in five minutes ! What d'ye
think of that now ! "

" Oh I say ! " expostulated Mr. Fanshawe, who
was obviously unused to being chaffed by elderly
ladies.

" Oh, 'pon me honour I did," returned Mrs. Fitz-
Symons, in her undulating brogue ; " but Gus here
wouldn't give me a stable, and I had to put the foal
in the potting shed, and he jumped out through the
window and destroyed himself with the broken glass.
Johnny put nineteen stitches in him, and he and I
were up two nights with him—the creature !—and
after all he wasn't a penny the worse ; but it isn't
every one has a vet on the premises, like me, Miss
Rowan ! "

She looked at the vet in question with a rallying
yet protective eye. John Michael's mother was
aware that her son did not distinguish himself socially,
and like Marlboro', who to fainting squadrons sent
the timely aid, was despatching Katharine to his
succour.

John Michael, on his music-stool, was but two yards away from Miss Rowan, weighed down by shyness palpable enough to touch a heart of stone. His red hands suggested icy ablutions at the pump in the yard ; his dark hair was plastered down as if with the stable water-brush ; he eyed Katharine from under his curling black eyelashes like a thing at bay. She felt that if so much as a twig cracked he would melt into the upright piano, even as Daphne was merged in the laurel.

" Have you got the colt still ? " she asked, addressing herself to what she hoped would be the line of least resistance.

John Michael's teaspoon fell from his saucer. " No we have not," he said to it and to the floor.

" I hope he had no other disaster ? " persevered Katharine.

" He had not ; we sold him."

" You ought to have charged extra for him as a piece of Art needlework ! " said Katharine, daringly, and found she had touched the right spot.

" Oh, he wasn't blemished at all," said John Michael quickly. " I sold him very well. I swapped him for thirty-four sovereigns and a harness-horse, and the man that got him sold him for seventy."

" Splendid ! " said Katharine.

There was a pause, during which Miss Rowan wondered if any process of arithmetic could sift out of this transaction the value of the harness-horse. The pause continued ; it was as though a feeble puff of wind had filled the sail and died again.

" Then I suppose you sold the harness-horse for thirty-five ? " ventured Katharine at length.

" We have him yet," said John Michael gravely. " He has a big knee."

Katharine became aware that she had pushed her success rather too far, and fell into a discouraged silence. There was another pause, during which she tried in vain to catch Mrs. Masterman's eye.

" I suppose you never were at Cahirmee ? " said John Michael, with an effort that wrung a creak from the music-stool.

Katharine felt that she was witnessing the awakening of a social conscience. It was unfortunate that she was obliged to answer the question in the negative.

" Well, it's a chancey place to buy a colt." He looked at her with something approaching to confidence in his hazel eyes, he even seemed on the verge of committing himself to a further statement, when the upheaval of departure fell upon the room. His mother saw the look, and said to herself with a mental pounce at what was, for her, the heart of the matter, " Ah, she'd never think of him ! "

In the motor, on the return journey, Mrs. Masterman and Katharine drew deep breaths of fresh air and relief, and, in the security of the tonneau, abandoned themselves, after the manner of guests, to untrammelled criticism of their entertainers and the friends of their entertainers.

" No," said Mrs. Masterman, decisively, " I have never before been in any part of Ireland where there was not so much as *one* white person. But I may candidly admit I don't ask for better company than Mrs. Fitz-Symons ! I saw you making very heavy weather of it with your handsome deaf mute."

" He's a nice gentle thing," said Katharine dictatorially. " When I die I'm going to endow a hospital for the Shy, and there shall be a John Michael ward."

" A lethal chamber would be more to the point," said Mrs. Masterman, " give me his mother, any day ! "

" All nice people are shy," proclaimed Katharine, and fell heavily into Mrs. Masterman's arms as the motor swung on two wheels into the main road,

CHAPTER VIII

IT was indisputable that the Widow Delanty
had retired, in a somewhat definite manner,
from her position of humble follower of the ladies
to whom she had attached herself at Aix. Yet
nothing was further from her intention than relinquishing her rights in them as Show-woman and
Patentee. If, indeed, she had exhibited a small
white fang at the Kennels, it had only been because
her rights in another and more ancient patent
had been infringed, and to Mrs. Delanty and her
class the baring of a fang is an affair of but passing
moment ; even a more serious passage of arms is
taken as part of any day's work, and makes no lasting
impression on those inured to combat.

Mrs. Delanty therefore continued to expound her
distinguished tenants to the neighbourhood, as one
who translates a classic into a speech understanded
of the people ; she also, and with a thrilling sense
of power, expounded the neighbourhood to her
distinguished tenants ; she appointed to the Lake-
View household its various purveyors ; she licensed
certain of the beggars to its charities, and gave the
necessary family details wherewith to confute the
undeserving ; she knew to an oat what Dermot had
and what he had not to eat. It was she who decided
that the next meet following on the visit to the
Kennels was too far away to be feasible.

" I wouldn't give that young fellow twelve miles
of the road. Better save him for the day when
they're meeting here."

It was under her expert guidance that Katharine
exercised " the young fellow," and incidentally learned
something of the lie of the coverts, something also
of the lies of the covert-keepers, and a great deal

about the implicit confidence placed by the Master
and the Huntsman in her information on such matters.
The widow was one of the administrators of the Fowl
Fund ; slowly, and by the medium of many circuitous
conversations at cottage doors, Katharine began to
apprehend it as a fitting school for diplomats, a
school in which no rules could be taught, and in
which every treaty was in its essence a compromise.
Mrs. Delanty, in these matters, showed an adroitness
and a grasp so entirely native that she was herself
unaware of them. She knew when to listen in silence,
she knew how to plant a question where it was least
desired, she knew how to bluster in a way that opened
Katharine's eyes to the unpleasant possibilities of the
art, she also knew when to pay and look pleasant.
Incidentally, Katharine made up her mind that it
would be neither wise nor agreeable to have any
financial difference of opinion with Mrs. Delanty.

Between these interviews they wandered through
much country, by the stony, twisting lanes and by-
roads with which it was veined. One of these Staff
Rides took them into a strange, inconsequent district
of grey and brown and purple hills, thrown about
among pasture and long streaks of bog ; nothing
was consistent, all was interrupted just as it was
beginning to have a character ; it was like three
countries broken up and mixed together, and of them
but one resembled a hunting country. For Mrs.
Delanty, however, it had no other aspect ; neither
hill-top nor boggy valley was without its legend,
scarcely a bank that could not boast of its casualty.
And through all wound the annals of the Young
Horses that she had ridden over it. To Miss Rowan
were displayed the precipices down which they had
floated, the boundary banks on which they had
disdained to " put an iron " ; the coped walls, on
the further side of which she had found herself " alone
with the hounds." Katharine listened respectfully,
hopelessly, and told herself, as many another stranger

in a strange country has done, that these things were, in all senses of the word, too high for her.

The widow, on this particular afternoon, was in search of a poultry-owner, whose cottage had been located by another poultry-owner as being "not the throw of your thumbnail from the new chapel." Armed with this information, she and Katharine jogged for a mile or so, upwards, into a sample of country that was bare and rocky, with the pale stone walls on either side of the road glistening from a shower, and the new chapel a notable land-mark in front, its grey roof nearly lost against an identical grey sky. In the chapel enclosure, among heaps of mortar and stones, stood the priest, big and black, in his soutane and biretta, a figure fraught with the romance of the religion that satisfies the poetical as well as the practical side of the Irish people. Black and big and powerful, and a friendly man at heart. It was Saturday, and he had been hearing confessions. A woman in a dark blue cloak was going forth again, shriven, into her world. Katharine wondered what sins she had been ingenious enough to commit in what appeared to be complete solitude. A bicycle leaned against the brand new gate, and a tall man in light grey clothes was talking to the priest, asking the way, judging by the explanatory gestures of the priest. The man lifted his cap and turned towards his bicycle.

"Why—isn't that——? " began Mrs. Delanty.

"Yes, it is!" said Katharine, smiting Dermot. "Hi! Stop! Mr. Adare!" She was suddenly aware that she felt as might a marooned seaman, who, surrounded by friendly natives, sees a man-o'-war's boat arrive at his coral beach.

" 'Dr. Livingstone, I presume'!" said Katharine, beaming upon him. "What an extraordinary place for you to turn up. I see you've actually changed your plans!"

"The picture-post-card did it. I wired to Jean from the station—I hope you don't mind?"

"It was a great liberty!" said Katharine, with a further realization of the feelings of the marooned seaman at being able again to speak his own language; had she spoken thus to John Michael, she thought, he would have fled at top speed.

Mrs. Delanty had pursued the woman with the blue cloak, and had departed with her towards the horizon, in search of the still invisible house that was "but the throw of a thumbnail" from the chapel.

"Is that the creature you spoke about as Dermot?" said Ulick Adare, regarding Katharine and her horse attentively, "or is Dermot the hero who pilots you and the hounds through these wildernesses? The Hymn of Praise that you wrote to me on the subject was a little confusing."

"This is Dermot," said Katharine, repressively, "I'm not responsible for the name. They said it was unlucky to change it, so I didn't."

"I've never seen you on a horse before," he said, looking at her with disfavour. "I don't think I like it. It turns you into a tailor's advertisement. And then that horrible hat; and your hair—like a door-knob—a nice, real gold door-knob of course,—but—still——"

"Oh, thank you!" said Katharine.

"Why must you wear these things? Every woman on horseback should be a pageant in herself; plumed hat—flowing skirt—touches of gold lace—And she should ride upon a white palfrey, with a silver mane and tail; not on a drab-coloured monster, cropped like a convict."

"You got out of that very well," said Katharine critically. "Not on a drab-coloured monster, cropped like a convict; 'it scans quite nicely!'"

"I'm glad to find you still retain some literary sentiment." He was leading his bicycle along the road beside her, and he turned as he spoke, and regarded her with grey-blue eyes that had the comrade's glance. "How's the book getting on? I suppose it has suddenly been transformed into a Sporting Novel—You and Dermot as hero and heroine, surrounded by a circle of yearning squireens."

"I particularly dislike the word yearn," said Katharine to Dermot's ears.

"Oh why? Very respectable people yearn."

"That makes it worse," retorted Katharine.

"As a matter of fact," he went on, "there's no such thing in literature as a Sporting Novel. The two things are incompatible."

"And why, pray?" challenged Katharine, who was argumentative by nature and by practice.

"Sport," said Adare, dogmatically, "is like Aaron's Serpent. It is the master passion in the breast, and it swallows all the rest. Sentiment, romance, character, even humour, they simply don't exist where sport is concerned. I've just come from a house where they hunted all day and talked about it all night. They used to debate for hours as to whether the fox ran one side of a furze bush or the other before the hounds devoured him."

"You confuse your smart hunting people with hunting," exclaimed Katharine, bursting in upon this homily. "Hunting is full of romance! I need not quote the poets to you! I leave it to your memory and your conscience!"

The trotting of Mrs. Delanty's horse here made itself heard. Ulick Adare looked back and prepared to mount his bicycle.

"Well, here's your heroine! I suppose she's full of romance too? Mind you give her a plumed hat; I'm not having any romance just now, I'm for tea. This is the way, isn't it?"

Katharine watched his long legs working like a knife grinder's, and reserved to herself the intention of telling him that people who ride bicycles had better be silent on the subject of romance.

E

CHAPTER IX

MISS ROWAN and Mr. Adare had known each other for two or three years, intermittently and unexactingly. It was a friendship that came forth with the summer days and the warm weather, and was laid up in the winter like a yacht. The existence of the friendship was due to a large extent to Mrs. Masterman, who had had a little house on the river near Hampton Court, and was lenient to friendships, even to what she held to be futile and impersonal ones.

They did indeed write to each other occasionally in the winter, and their letters were highly creditable, and betokened a mutual respect for each other's appreciation; Ulick Adare, in fact, sometimes, when he had literary work in view, utilized a letter to Katharine as a preliminary canter for his ideas. Jean Masterman, in her unregenerate and practical heart, said to herself that not thus had her young men written to her what time she had been a combatant and said Ha! Ha! among the Captains, but, being a large-minded person, she accepted the possibility of other methods, and wrote to her William (who, at the moment, was at Pindi), that it seemed to her it all came to the same thing in the long run.

This state of things had been arrived at during idle, serene afternoons on the river, and in high, still mornings amid blue and silver Swiss mountains; the personal note had not been touched in it, or not more than was inevitably in two people who had cultivated their self-consciousness by much reading of the later poets. Summer, and the silences of the river and the mountains, had imparted the needful vibration of sentiment; the friendship that could maintain its vibrating quality in one of Mrs. Delanty's

" occasional chairs " in front of a meagre Lake View fire-place, would need to be of a hardier constitution.

But this was not a mere matter of background. The fair and pleasing being, restful and appreciative with her grey eyes shaded by a languidly-curving straw hat, and sufficiently reserved to have a tinge of mystery about her, was not the Katharine whom Adare found at Lake View in November. This later Katharine came down to breakfast in her habit, robustly determined to exercise her horse at 10 o'clock; irrespective of other people's plans or designs; preoccupied about the stuffing of her saddle, indignant over the misfits of Tim's corduroys. Worst of all, she was cheery, a metallic, cold-weather quality, very unsuitable to a vibrating friendship.

" How long are you going to stay here ? " he demanded of his cousin, as, through a window blurred with rain, they saw Katharine returning at speed to the stable, after a two-hours' excursion.

" As long as it suits the children, and Katharine doesn't get bored," replied Mrs. Masterman ; " it may be nasty, but it is certainly cheap, and that, my dear, is a point worthy of consideration, though you may not think so ! "

" Don't I, though ! " said Ulick Adare, morosely. " Anyhow, I don't think you need be anxious about Miss Rowan."

The door opened, and Katharine appeared, dripping and glowing, radiating an entirely discordant healthfulness and good temper.

" Such a day ! " she said. " But it was rather delicious, too ! I suppose you two wasters haven't moved from the fire since I saw you ! This room feels like an oven ! "

" Go ! go ! You horrible creature ! " exclaimed Mrs. Masterman, " you're dripping over everything ! I *like* ovens ! "

The door was banged.

" This climate is certainly the place for com-
plexions ! " said Jean Masterman to her cousin.
" Did you ever see a more lovely colour ? "

" A high colour is death to expression," replied
Mr. Adare, sourly.

The meet at Lake View, next day, was a matter
that had been specially arranged for the glorification
of the most recent subscriber to the hunt. A thrill
pervaded the establishment, in unconscious response
to that commanding quality that the Chase exercises
without an effort over all within its scope. The
Pomeranian was immured in a bedroom, where it
squeaked and scratched with the indignation of a
caged lion and the pertinacity of a mechanical toy.
The kitchenmaids' mother, who came to sell chickens,
found herself famous on announcing that the fox
had whipped two from her ere yesterday. En-
thusiastically cross-examined by Miss Rowan, she
became expansive, and declared that he was in it
always. It wasn't a week since she met him back
in the hill, " and he eating a goose. And the goose
screeching, and he having a puss on him that long "—
—(the kitchenmaid's mother here extended a wiry
arm and swiftly indicated the length between her
elbow and her wrist)—" the merry rogue ! "

It was Ulick Adare who explained to Katharine
that it was the length of the fox's jaw that had been
defined, and thereby found himself for a few moments, as it were, in the picture. That was at 10.45.
At 11 he was again wholly outside it.

" Four red coats ! " said Mrs. Delanty, standing
in the sunshine at the open hall-door, looking as
spruce as a little black bird. " Quite a smart meet !
They'll be all on the ride to-day ! they know they
can trust *our* coverts, Mrs. Masterman ! "

She looked round her approvingly, noting the
suitable array of restoratives set forth on a table,
feeling that even the tall, immaculate parlourmaid
redounded to her personal credit.

"Mr. Fanshawe has motored an X.H. man over with him. I told him this was a sure find!"

Outside, on the limited gravel sweep, John Michael sat solemnly in the middle of his hounds and rejected all refreshment. The smart meet, some twenty in number, straggled in the narrow drive, and overflowed into the more congenial stableyard. Shy young men in nondescript attire, and on horses that equally defied classification, coyly, and with mantling blushes, accepted drinks from the coldly composed English parlourmaid. In the hall Ulick Adare, artistically conscious of his position outside the picture, of his tame, unheroic shooting clothes, of his wool-clad calves, with their inherent suggestion of trudging afoot, plied among the fox-hunters with a creditable assumption of old-fashioned hospitality. Even Mr. Fitz-Symons, concocting for himself a tall and mahogany-coloured whisky-and-soda, with his sallow, vulgar face and over-filled waistcoat, borrowed bravery from his attire, so ancient, so potent is the gallantry of the red coat, the white breeches, the spurred boots. Young Fanshawe, whose inmost soul was swimming in a sea of glory, because of the indisputable superiority of his breeches over those of all others at the meet, chaffed Mrs. Delanty with loud, slow inanity; and Mrs. Delanty, delicately sipping her tiny glass of sloe-gin, answered a fool according to his folly, and felt that she was, as her sister had said to her that very morning, "moving in circles."

Unlike Mrs. Delanty, Miss Rowan was not enjoying herself. The gilt had suddenly and inexplicably taken its departure from the gingerbread. She felt chilly and pessimistic; nauseated by the Master, exasperated by Mrs. Delanty and her swains. She was aware of an intense and dreary aloofness from the babbling crew that surrounded her. She wondered if she were going to be ill; she wondered if she were going to be killed. That, she decided,

was it. She was going to be killed ! This
mood was a portent, and having made up her mind
to this she felt a little better. She thought about
her will, and remembered that Dermot was not mentioned in it. Should she rush upstairs and write a
codicil, leaving him to Jean ? She was restrained
by the reflection that there were few things that
Jean would more entirely dislike. With this she
even laughed a little, and feeling still better went
out and talked to John Michael, sitting on the chestnut mare in the middle of his hounds. By the time
she had extorted from him the information that he
had sixteen and a half couple out, and had, after
three failures, identified Dauntless, she had abandoned the idea of the codicil. There was an eminent
sanity about John Michael, something so solidly
anti-neurotic, that he almost amounted to a tonic.

The hounds moved off at last—Mr. Fitz-Symons
was on these occasions a bad starter—and Katharine
mounted her horse, and found that, in honour, no
doubt, of the visitors, her saddle had been polished
till it felt like glass. She also found that there was
something like a rudimentary camel's hump beneath
it.

" He's getting up his back a bit ! " said Dermot's
late owner ranging up beside Katharine on her staid
bay mare, " but he doesn't know how to buck."

" I think he's anxious to learn," said Katharine,
in jerks, holding Dermot with a beginner's convulsive
clutch, as he curvetted round the stern of an outside
car. " I've never known him so—so *brutally* fresh as
before ! "

" That boy is giving him too much to eat, and I
told you that before ! Keep with me, he'll go quietly
with his old friend here. You should see this lady
with one on her that isn't up to her tricks ! *She's*
the girl to buck ! "

" She doesn't buck as big as her rider ! " said Mr.
Clery, who was a humorist, to his young friend, Mr.

Doyle, as they rode behind the ladies, observing all things.

The procession here left the road, and had the pleasant grass been hot lava, Miss Rowan's steed could hardly have evinced more agitation.

" The hill will steady him," said Mr. Doyle sympathetically to Katharine ; "there'll not be much chat out of him once he gets to the top o' that ! "

It was the selfsame hill up whose heights John Michael had so nimbly fled from the interrupted house-warming at Lake View.

" Very little that horse'll mind the hill, I can tell you ! " said Mrs. Delanty, scornfully. " But you'll see they'll not find there. I got a sure word that fox is keeping my covert this while back."

Mrs. Delanty liked Jimmy Doyle about as well as he liked her—which is a more usual measure of affection than is generally admitted—and being proprietor, as it were, of Katharine, of Dermot, and of the hill, had no intention of allowing him, as she said to herself, " to poke his nose in where it wasn't wanted."

A ploughed field came next, a boggy one, of a nature absorbent to superfluous equine energy ; Katharine felt the proud Dermot flounder ingloriously in the furrows, and trusted that there might be many more ploughed fields, and deep ones. The hounds and their huntsman had already crossed it ; the Master stopped short at the gateway and looked menacingly at his followers. The advance ceased guiltily, and young Fanshawe and his friend, who were leading, fell back in good order.

" I'd take it as a favour if the conversaziony were held in the furzy field back ! " said Mr. Fitz-Symons, who had perfected his particular vein of sarcasm in many a Petty Sessions Court, " as agreeable as you are, I don't think the fox'll be apt to stay in the hill to listen to ye ! "

" Don't look so frightened ! " said Mrs. Delanty

to Mr. Fanshawe. "That's nothing! He's always as cross as the cats on a hunting morning!"

The Field withdrew with the philosophy and the impenitence of Fields, and the Master rode on slowly in the wake of the hounds, now trotting lightly across a grass field towards the covert. John Michael pulled off his shabby cap, and with a sudden cheer loosed them at the towering side of the hill; they stormed over the stony bank that lay between them and it, and were immediately lost to sight in its mantle of furze. Their huntsman slipped off his mare, summoned by name one of the fortuitous retinue of runners, and dived after the hounds into the prickly depths.

Then ensued a long period of inaction, for which none of Katharine's studies in fox-hunting literature had at all prepared her. There was a warmth in the sun, as is the wont of winter suns in the south-west of Ireland; there was warm colour on the hillside, and flecks of yellow here and there in the gorse. There was a blue sky with white clouds in it, and the sweetness of trodden grass was in the moist air, but the artistic Miss Rowan's cultivated mind was engrossed in other and quite unaesthetic aspects of her surroundings. The hill-side faced her oppressively, full of problems insoluble to her. If the hounds went away at the top how was anyone to follow them? She perused the cattle-tracks and lost them in clumps of furze, or marked them to a full-stop at out-crops of cliff. Tom Coyne, on his cunning old chestnut screw, was on the sky-line (happy and marvellous Tom Coyne!), but how he had arrived there was known only to himself. Mrs. Delanty must, of course, be in the secret, thought the perturbed Katharine; how, otherwise, could she maintain an apparently cheerful conversation with Mr. Fanshawe, while at each moment the hounds were moving further on upwards. Silence prevailed along the hill-front, except where John

Michael's voice rose in apostrophe to the hounds ; he himself was invisible, save when his black cap or red coat-sleeve showed above the furze as he struggled after them. Looking behind her, Katharine saw Jean Masterman with her kodak, and Ulick Adare with his bicycle, waiting on the road. They were creatures of another world, quite wanting in greatness, or even significance, yet she was not so remote that she did not presently perceive with fitting satisfaction the spectacle of Mrs. Masterman being hauled, by the hand of Eily, on to the outside car of Eily and her boon companions.

A chilly quarter of an hour elapsed ; Katharine fell again into speculation upon her probably early death, and asked herself if the world contained another method of wasting time, money, and possibly life, as complete as fox-hunting.

"There's some hounds out on the top," said Jimmy Doyle, suddenly.

Everyone stopped talking and stared at a few specks that crept like white ants up a track near the crest of the hill.

"I think I'll go and see what they're at," continued Mr. Doyle, in his small, incredibly discreet voice, gathering up his reins.

Katharine looked for guidance to Mrs. Delanty.

"That's nothing but a stale line," said her preceptress, airily. "I dare say he went out of that an hour ago."

All, nevertheless, moved forward. Two fields away the Master turned and pursued at a heavy trot a course parallel with the hill.

"There's the Master started," said young Fanshawe, throwing away his cigarette, and hustling his horse at a confronting bank. "About time for us to get a move on us."

"That's a bad landing," said Mrs. Delanty, quickly, to Katharine, holding her mare tightly, "come this way."

Katharine attempted to obey and Dermot instantly got up on his hind legs.

"Let him have the bank," said Jimmy Doyle, as he followed Fanshawe.

His black mare changed feet on it, with her manner of the perfect servant, and sank out of sight.

"Bit of a drop," called back her rider.

"My turn next!" said Dermot, tearing his head free from Katharine's chilled fingers. He struck off with a couple of eager bounds, and in his youthful arrogance flew the fence from field to field.

"Fled it, b' George," said Mr. Clancy. "That's dangerous! Well rode, missy!"

As a matter of fact, it was not till Dermot landed, on all four feet, that the question of coming off presented itself to "missy;" it then, undoubtedly, became what might be termed a hanging matter, but Dermot had not been hogged, a comfortable fact, which turned the verdict in favour of the rider.

In the next field the Master had pulled up and was bellowing to the hillside, where now nothing whatever was visible.

"Keep up the hill," shouted Jimmy Doyle, making for a seemingly perpendicular channel in the furze. "I saw Johnny going away over the top in a hurry!"

Several others followed him, and with this the electric current was switched on. It was with the feeling that a life or death choice was presented to her that Katharine looked from them to the Master, a choice that had to be instant and might be irrevocable, her heart was going like a drum, and she had quite forgotten the probability of her early death.

"It's no good going up there," said Mrs. Delanty, appearing beside her with the suddenness of the Red Queen, and deciding the question. "There's a way up further on that's twice better than this! Keep on after the Master."

Mr. Fitz-Symons on his big brown horse had started again, and with elbows up and coat-tails flying was galloping with the utmost determination for the nearest gap. Katharine, Mrs. Delanty, and the two red coats pounded in his wake. As much as she could think of anything beyond the effort to hold her horse, she marvelled at the skill with which the master piloted them from gap to gap. She had yet to learn that there is a hunting memory for gaps, comparable only to the card-memory for the lesser trumps, that is bestowed by a kind providence on those who fitly appreciate it.

Mrs. Delanty, going easily beside her, assured her that there was no hurry, that the hounds weren't really running, that the way to hold a horse was give and take, and that if you trusted to Jimmy Doyle you might find yourself the Dear knows where. Who the Dear might be there was no time to inquire ; Katharine was only aware that they had now been steered into a cart-track, that the ruts were deep and that Dermot's neck had turned to iron. Where they were going, or what was happening, she did not know ; if this were a run she thought it highly unpleasant and quite unmeaning. Mr. Fitz-Symons was now dashing through a farmyard, with hens and geese in shrieking flight round him, cur-dogs barking hysterically, and, somewhere in the background, a mother slamming a half-door upon a flock of children ; then came a squeeze round the end of a gate, immovably ajar in the mud, and then they were all but on to a stony road that elbowed its way up and over the hill in which was still hidden the secret of the hounds. With stones flying, and horses beginning to blow, the quintette galloped furiously up the road, headed by the Master and Mrs. Delanty, between whom a strange alliance had manifested itself.

It was at about this juncture that the first flash of doubt of her leaders shot, like a flicker of neuralgia, through the soul of Katharine. They were nearing the top of the hill, green fields were spreading on either side, why then continue to career along a road like a riding-school gone mad ?

A similar flicker had apparently assailed Mr. Fanshawe.

"I'm damned if I know what we're at ! " he said to his comrade red-coat, " busting along a road like this for nothing ! "

The comrade replied, with suitable vigour of language, that they had made an error of judgment in not having gone up the hill at first.

"Well, I've had enough of this rot," said Mr. Fanshawe, leaving the riding-school ranks abruptly, and facing his reluctant and well-blown horse at the bank by the roadside. "They're bound to be somewhere this way."

His comrade did likewise, and the remnant of the road-riders swept on, leaving behind them the displeasing conflict between indignant horses and angry men.

It was a level ground now, a table-land at the top of the hill. The Master pulled up, and he and his attendant ladies paused, with the horses' sides going and their tails twitching, while the sun shone down upon them and their anxieties in complete leisure and unconcern. A quarter of a mile away there were two men standing on a fence.

"There they are ! " exclaimed Mrs. Delanty, discovering the greater in the less in defiance of Euclid, " and they're not hunting ! I knew that stale line was nonsense."

Far away to the left a red-coated rider was moving towards them slowly. Mr. Fitz-Symons snatched at his horn and blew several long and fierce blasts upon it.

"Now you see how nicely we've hit them off ! " said the widow to her dubious disciple, " instead of killing the horses for nothing over that hill !

Poor Dermot's carrying a good two stone more
now than he ever had to do with poor little
me ! "

Not a hair of Mrs. Delanty's head had moved
from its set place, her colour had deepened but
had also remained within its proper sphere ; she
had an indisputably neat seat on a horse.

" Oh, for goodness sake, look at poor Fanshawe !
The short cut didn't thrive with him ! "

That ardent youth was now returning to the road;
a process apparently as difficult as leaving had been.
There was a green stain on the knee of his breeches,
and mud on his horse's shoulder ; it was obvious
that the period of his absence had not been devoid
of incident. Three fields away his companion's
head appeared and disappeared periodically above
the line of a fence, like a revolving light, in corre-
spondence, presumably with the refusals of his horse.

John Michael, with his following, was by this time
within hail, advancing in silence, accepting his step-
brother's loud and full-bodied criticisms upon his
intellect and capacity with the callousness learned
in the House of Bondage.

Mrs. Delanty winked at Katharine ; the wink
ricocheted off the flinty impassivity of Miss Rowan's
expression and found its mark in Mr. Fanshawe;
who giggled responsively. Katharine, with grey
eyes as clear and expressionless as a cat's, looked
straight in front of her, and Mrs. Delanty became
suddenly aware of a quality in her protégé that she
had not before encountered. She regretted the
wink, though it seemed to her to express to a nicety
her own entire yet lenient grasp of the position.
" Tout comprendre, c'est tout pardonner," that was
what the wink said. After all (as she would have
said to Katharine, if Katharine's furious soul had
been revealed to her) it was the only fun old Gus
got out of the hunting—this swaggering and shouting
and cursing John Michael and everybody. And

Johnny—she thought of him as Johnny—wasn't
such a fool as to mind ; he knew well enough that
he had all the fun and Gus did all the paying.

CHAPTER X

"IT was a fox right enough," said John Michael,
in ultimate reply to his brother, "they
couldn't carry him on, but I think he's not far off.
They cried it to Mahony's bounds. I was casting
them when you blew the horn."

"Well, you can cast them on to the road now, and
keep them there till you get to Mrs. Delanty's plan-
tation," answered the Master, "I'm not going on
with any of your damned stale lines ! "

It seemed to Katharine that the power of money
over the money-less could not be more nakedly set
forth.

The words were scarcely uttered when that which
is most suitably known in Ireland as "a screech"
broke from the two men on the distant fence. The
hounds sprang to attention ; there was another
screech, barbed with the uncomparable frenzy of
those in the act of viewing a fox, and they were
gone, like greyhounds from the slips.

"For'rad ! For'rad ! For'rad ! " yelled John
Michael, transformed in one second into a deaf maniac.
Had he not been both, he could hardly have ignored
the bellow that commanded him to hold hard, and
not to make a fool of the hounds, to—here even Mr.
Fitz-Symons' remarks were drowned in the whoop
in which Mr. Fanshawe released his soul, and, maniac
as John Michael, stormed in pursuit of him over the
wall that separated the road from the hill.

"Now for it ! " said Dermot to Katharine, hurtling

over the wall hard on the heels of Mr. Fanshawe's
chestnut.

Katharine heard the inevitable voice of her preceptress calling after her.

" That's a dangerous thing to do ! "

But she was in a new world and Mrs. Delanty was
outside it. It was a limited world, containing but one
idea. Never again, while life lasted, to let the hounds
get out of her sight. The idea was shared by Dermot,
which simplified matters in many ways, if not in all.
Another wall occurred ; round, loose stones, rising
from the short mountainy grass, and she knew for
the first time the glory of feeling a big horse jumping
big out of his stride ; other riders were there, pelting
in front of her, beside her, thundering after her ; the
bang-tail of John Michael's mare held her eye. She
thought, " If I lose sight of it for an instant I'm done
for ! " It did not seem to her at all absurd. Ulick
Adare had assured her only the day before that the
cessation of self-consciousness indicates the return
to the savage state, and that pure emotion is always
primitive : she had responded with an equal affecta-
tion that she liked savages, and preferred them
slightly stupid. This, he told her, only betrayed
her supreme effeteness. She was now as frankly a
savage as she could have wished, and was unaware
of it, which brought her even nearer to her own
ideal.

She was coming at the bank on which the men had
been standing, she was over it without either thought
or volition ; the men were still ahead, running,
shouting, gesticulating.

" It was beyond under the rock he was lying ! "
shrieked one of them. " The Villyan ! Dhrive on
your dogs into the smell ! "

" They have it ! They have it ! " shrieked the
other. He stuck his hands together, his face scarlet,
his eyes blazing. Whatever the madness of the
chase may be, he too was possessed by it.

A clash as from a steeple-full of bells shook the air ; the hounds snatched at the line, a big white and yellow dog-hound drove out to the front with his head up, vociferating.

" 'Leu ! Trumpeter, boy ! Trumpeter ! " cried his huntsman, in a rapture of love, his voice piercing the din ; " get to Trumpeter there ! " The hounds crushed in together, as if they were squeezing through a narrow gateway, they lengthened out into a stream, they fleeted, they sped, and the river of their music flowed back to Katharine and she galloped in it, and there was nothing else in Heaven or earth.

Along the level grassy crest of the hill the hounds ran, and certain things were revealed to the novice. Primarily that Dermot was not pulling, also that hounds did not get very far away from those who kept close to John Michael, and also, but this discovery she did not make till the first check, that among the dozen riders who were in it, were *not* the Master and Mrs. Delanty. These things, however, were beside the point ; the central fact was that she was there, and the Primitive Hunter, who is at the back of all ancestries, was shouting the fact into her ear, as she sat, panting, and drove in hairpins, while hats were straightened, and ties shoved in, and one red face beamed upon another in that sudden, soul-to-soul comradeship that is oblivious of complexion. How terrible, yet how improving, to overhear, at such a moment, Jimmy Doyle murmur to a colleague buckeen :

" Keep clear of her at the bank—she was into the small of my back at the last place. That horse jumps very quick ! "

Katharine moved slowly away, stricken to the core of her vain-glory, and immediately the hounds broke forth into their straining cry, and her heart jumped up again into her throat, and all was forgotten. The country that lies like a map before the calm observer, again began to rush at her in a series of disjointed problems ; here was a bank with rotten ground in front of it, over which the hounds skimmed like swallows ; while the riders must swing aside and scramble in single file up and through a mire-choked cattle gap ; it was agony to wait her turn, and feel that hounds and huntsman were at each moment further away ; ecstacy to hear the heavy brogue of some philanthropist, adjuring his fellows to " Let the lady through ! " Ecstacy again to feel her horse gather himself for an extra effort and gain on the leaders. They were turning off the hill now and heading downwards through pale fields with sheep in them, and over thick loose walls on which the wiser horses changed feet clatteringly ; not so Dermot, who, with the fall of ground, was beginning again to get the better of his rider and was lessening at each jump the space she endeavoured to preserve between him and the small of Mr. Doyle's back. With what felt like her last ounce of strength she wrenched him out of the direct wake of the black mare, and landed, much disorganised, elbow to elbow with the black mare's rider in a marshy field, a flat, heaven-sent field, in which the horses were at once over their fetlocks.

They had arrived at the floor of a wide valley; fifty yards ahead the hounds were flitting to and fro in front of a long line of rushes. Jimmy Doyle leaned over and laid his hand on Katharine's reins.

" Hold on awhile ; he might have run up this side of it." ("This side of *what ?* " thought Katharine.) " No, by Jove ! He's across after all ! Now the fun will begin."

As he spoke, one hound after the other rose into the air as if pitched up from a spring-board. They were jumping something wide.

" That's the Kael ! " said Jimmy Doyle, and looked at Miss Rowan with a peculiar grin.

" Why ? " she said, answering the grin.

F

" You'll see that ! " said Jimmy Doyle, beginning
to go.

John Michael was trotting fast along the verge
of what had now declared itself to be a wide drain,
full from black edge to black edge with sleepy bog
water. It was not a country of water-jumps, and
in any country the Kael as a water-jump would have
commanded respect. John Michael scanned the
boggy take-off and the unprepossessing landing.

" Bad's the best ! " he called back. Then pulling
back from the drain some twenty yards through the
marshy grass, he drove the chestnut mare at it with
the sudden fire that is special and personal, like
" attack " in music. Her wild eye told that she was
afraid of the water, but her faithful heart kindled
with John Michael's. Water-jumping was not her
branch of the art, but to his shout she responded,
and with an effort she rose high at it as if it were
a wall, and got over with but little to spare. As she
landed her rider looked round quickly.

" Tom, you'd better show Miss Rowan the way
round by the bridge on Carthy's land."

" Sure it's half a mile to the bridge," said Tom
Coyne, sourly. " Try would he jump it, Miss."

Fanshawe's chestnut had already refused twice,
very heartily ; Jimmy Doyle was over, by main
strength, that is to say by flinging himself off on to
the further bank, and dragging his receding mare
out by the mouth, like a fish. Katharine obeyed
Tom Coyne, but without conviction, a fact immediately appreciated by Dermot. He rushed at the water
with deceitful speed, then with an equal speed
turned and fled from it. This he did several times,
with growing enthusiasm ; one of the farmers got
across, and Mr. Fanshawe and his horse fell in.
Other riders started for the bridge, and Katharine
and Dermot continued their dismal pas-seul on the
trampled banks of the Kael.

" It'd be as good for us to go on out of this, Miss,"

said Tom Coyne, fretting at the delay, yet with a humorous eye on the unhappy Fanshawe, who, dripping with bog-stuff, was holding his horse's head above water till help should arrive. "There's plenty will be glad to earn a shilling pulling him out that has more time to spare than ourselves! Faith, the gentleman that came with him is worse than him! He's in up to his girths in a bog back on Knockcoora!"

The bridge was more than half a mile away, all bridges are, under such circumstances. To Katharine it seemed like ten miles, by the end of the leaden-hearted gallop that brought them to it. The glow and the inspiration were gone ; the Primitive Hunter, with his rudimentary tail between his legs, was experiencing the seamy side of hunting. But there still remained Tom Coyne, to whom glows and inspirations were as nothing. The hounds had passed out of existence, yet he neither stopped nor stayed. It was all dark to Katharine as the science of navigation or the deductions of the Augurs ; cattle, loose horses, crows yielded instruction to Tom Coyne ; human beings, invisible to her, were hailed at their standpoint in space as " Young fella ' ! " and their incomprehensible replies translated into action. He took the best place in each fence as inevitably as water takes the line of least resistance, and Miss Rowan in suicidal depression, and momently becoming stiffer, followed him abjectly.

They had progressed thus for a mile or so, when a solitary hound was manifested on the top of a fence. Tom Coyne stood up in his stirrups and roared at it, and cracked his whip like a pistol-shot. " Get forrad, Amazon ! " he yelled.

" We have them now, Miss ! " he said, with the mildness of one who is greater than his triumph ; " there might be some worse than us yet ! "

Following the line of Amazon's flight, Katharine saw afar off, John Michael and three or four other riders crossing a road and struggling up a hill towards a clump of fir trees. There was a patch of white among the fir trees.

"They have him to ground!" said Tom Coyne, spurring his tired horse.

There was a red coat in the trees among the hounds, and a lady on horseback was holding a horse beside them.

"Well, that beats the bees in the making of wax!" said Tom Coyne, jumping into the road.

On the road was the outside car of Eily, and from Eily and her companions a chorus of squeals, as of questing plover, arose, announcing to Katharine that they had seen the whole run, that no road was too rough for them, that they always stuck to the Master, that they had just met Mr. Fanshawe's friend——! Here the whole party became incoherent with laughter, still plover-like.

At this juncture Katharine became aware of Mr. Adare approaching at a high rate of speed on his bicycle.

"I've seen the fox, I've seen the hounds, and I've seen the Master and Mrs. Delanty, at the top of the hunt!" he said, dismounting, and addressing Miss Rowan with a tranquillity of manner somewhat at variance with the speed of his approach. "They told me they were the only people in it, and that you had gone all wrong and were probably at the bottom of the river; I was going to look for you."

"Quite unnecessary, thanks," said Katharine, who found his tone elder-brotherly and resented it. "I think I'll go on and see what's happening up there."

She trotted on towards the hill, and left him to escape as best he might from the proffered sandwiches of Eily and her party.

CHAPTER XI

MISS ROWAN, seated at tea, with muddy riding boots, a pot hat on the back of her head, and a poached egg on her plate, was still in the savage state, and was boring her hearers with the simplicity of a Red Indian brave. The ignominious finish of her hunt was forgotten, and glory flowed from her. Fence by fence went the narrative; higher and higher leaped Dermot, more and more incomprehensible grew the tangle of the geography, and through all went, like the Great Twin Brethren, the mighty presences of John Michael and Jimmy Doyle.

Ulick Adare, lying back in his chair at the other end of Mrs. Masterman's hearthrug, listened to the Saga in the misanthropic silence that might be expected from a non-hunting male, who finds himself playing the attentive Desdemona to the adventureful Othello of a breezy and booted female. Miss Rowan had brought back with her something of the largeness of windy hilltops, and the farness of wide skies was in her face ; she had been dealing with primeval things, danger, and speed, and the face of nature, and the chase, which is near the heart of nature, and had dealt with them as a man among men. Ulick Adare, who had a no less comfortable conceit of himself than other young men, found the part of Desdemona not at all to his taste. It was a certain solace to stand with his back to the fire, and feel that he was six feet high, and had long straight legs, but it was preposterous that Katharine's limpid grey eyes should deepen and glow when she talked of one of these cave-dwellers jumping a bog drain.

Mrs. Masterman, smoking a philosophic cigarette

in one of the more reliable of the Delanty armchairs, was entirely aware of the position, and found it entertaining. That the sense of humour, on which her two young friends so specially plumed themselves, should at this juncture have deserted them both, was a matter that she could dilate on pleasurably in her next letter to William. William hunted, too, but he would understand.

"Your friend, John Michael, certainly looks his very best when he's riding," she said reflectively. "He reminds me of a native cavalryman; he has just their peculiar light, close seat on a horse."

Miss Rowan rose to the fly with pathetic simplicity. "His riding is a revelation!" she said solemnly.

"The Revelation of St. John-Michael the Divine!" said Ulick Adare to the widow Delanty's invalided drawing-room clock.

Katharine got out of her chair with as much dignity as was possible for a person to whom every change of position was an anguish.

"I must go out and see that Dermot is all right," she said very professionally, moving to the door with a gait suggestive of wooden legs.

"If you don't have a hot bath soon," said Mrs. Masterman, "you'll have to go to bed in your habit."

Dermot's owner made no reply; her departing footsteps lumbered slowly through the hall.

"I suppose I ought to have offered to go too," said Mr. Adare, as he closed the door behind her.

"My dear," said Mrs. Masterman, "she doesn't want you. That's part of the game. She wouldn't yield that privilege for worlds."

Ulick Adare sat down and occupied himself with a picture paper.

"How long do you suppose this obsession will last?" he said presently.

Mrs. Masterman was smocking something for her youngest born, and regarded her handiwork meditatively.

" For ever," she replied, selecting another coloured silk, and threading her needle with tranquil dexterity.

" That's a cheerful look-out for her friends ! "

" This acute phase won't last, you know," returned Mrs. Masterman ; " she'll learn to reserve it for her fellow maniacs."

" Fellow maniacs ! " repeated Mr. Adare, getting up and kicking the fire. " Vulgar people are never mad ! "

" That's rather interesting," said Mrs. Masterman. " But I should put it the other way, and say that mad people are never vulgar. But I don't call John Michael mad, or vulgar either. He's just a savage —a handsome savage, and I rather like the creature, apart from his looks," she added, placing a careful stitch and reviewing her company of little pleats.

Ulick Adare put his hands in his pockets and looked at her down his nose, and put on his manner of the Spectator office.

" I shall write an essay upon the blighting effect of needlework on the female mind. I have yet to meet the woman whom it does not deteriorate. They become prim and pragmatical, unspontaneous and self-sufficing."

" Dear, dear ! " said his cousin.

" A woman is a comrade when she smokes a cigarette," he went on, unaware that even as he fulminated he was yielding to that provoking quality in the needleworker that makes her desired as an audience—the restful quality of something at anchor. " She is bereft of either soul or sympathy when she's fumbling among reels of cotton and secretly looking for the scissors ! "

" Is it worse than hunting ? " suggested Mrs. Masterman.

" Not perhaps so absolutely obliterating to the intellect, but more detrimental to companionship."

Mrs. Masterman folded up her needlework and put it neatly away in its basket.

"My child," she said, "we have just twenty
minutes before it is time to dress. Sit down and let
us abuse them all comfortably. Bags I Mrs. Delanty."

CHAPTER XII

A MILE and a half away the lady of Mrs.
Masterman's selection was hurrying through
a routine familiarized by experience. With her own
small and thoroughly capable hands she had made
a bran mash, a matter requiring both method and
muscle ; she had bandaged the bay mare's legs
as deftly and firmly as a hospital nurse, and while
doing so had told Dinny the stable boy that there
had been a great hunt ; that the mare had never
put a foot wrong, and had been the first up when
the fox went to ground ; and Dinny the stable-boy
had rejoined politely :

"I wouldn't doubt her, ma'am," even though he
was as well aware as his employer of what had
occurred.

Having taken off her habit she had paid a final
visit to the stable to make sure that all was well.
Then, and not till then, did the Widow Delanty,
by this time a very tired little widow, permit herself
to sit down in the kitchen and partake of a cup of
tea. She chose the kitchen because it was warm,
and also because from it she could still influence for
good the all-important affairs of the stable-yard.

The person who supplied her with tea did not do so
without reproaches.

"It's a shame for you, Lily ! Look at the tea;
and it's as black as the pots with the way you have
it waiting on you ! "

"I don't care what colour it is, I'm dead from

the want of it!" answered Mrs. Delanty, expanding-comfortably into her native tongue, and helping herself to the buttered toast that her elder sister took out of the oven.

Enormous are the advantages of those that have meals in the kitchen ; the buttered toast bubbled on its plate, the black and broken-nosed teapot gushed forth its steaming flood with a freedom unknown to its drawing-room relative ; the steady glow of the range enveloped the widow's frozen little person. She had ridden home at a walk, as was her careful custom, and seven miles at a walk on a chilly November evening is, as Miss Janetta Scanlan was wont to say, " no laughing joke at all."

Miss Scanlan and Mrs. Delanty were, respectively the eldest and the youngest products of one of those prolific middle-class unions which are, we are assured, the props and stays of the realm. In whatever manner the realm may have benefited by the addition to it of eighteen Scanlans, it is quite certain that the eldest daughter of the house had found her brethren neither props nor stays. In Miss Janetta Scanlan's youth, education, especially for females, was deemed a superfluity, and the family talent for marriage not being bestowed upon her, she had spent her life as unpaid nursery maid, unpaid dressmaker, and unpaid sick nurse to her relations. Having no money she had no influence, standing or significance, a discreditable state of things not peculiar to Miss Scanlan's class or country, though being Ireland, good nature and family feeling entered into the matter more than they might have done elsewhere. Now, as cook, lady's maid, and upper housemaid to her sister Delanty, she was in what she felt to be the zenith of her ambitionless career. Lily's yoke was considerably lighter than that of her sister-in-law, Mrs. Joseph, or Mrs. Michael, or Mrs. Jeremiah Scanlan, with all of whom she had, in her time, partaken of the bread of affliction and the

water of affliction, and Lily's looks, her social success,
and her horsemanship, were articles of her pro-
foundest belief. When Lily lost her temper, which
she did frequently and thoroughly, her elder sister
regarded it as one of the privileges of a settled income,
and felt herself more than repaid when she was
permitted to put on her "Sunday dress" and join
with Mrs. Fitz-Symons or Captain Bolger in devouring
the hot cakes that she herself had compounded.

"Where's Kate?" said Mrs. Delanty, her practised
eye swiftly taking in all the details of the kitchen."

"Out milking the cow."

"A nice time to be milking at half-past six!"
commented Kate's mistress. "Did she darn those
stockings for me?"

"No, I did them myself," said Miss Scanlan,
who cherished for Kate the General an illicit sympathy
born of arduous fellow-service. "You were saying
that poor Dermot was going grand with the young
lady?"

"He was doing what he liked with her, if you call
that grand!" said Mrs. Delanty, relinquishing for
the moment the misdeeds of Kate, but by no means
forgetting them. "I'm sorry now I sold him to
her. A steady old crock, that's what she wants—
it's all she's fit for, anyhow!"

"I suppose she was following you all day?" said
the faithful Janetta.

"She thought she'd do better running after John
Michael and Jimmy Doyle, and believe me, they had
enough of her before the day was out!" replied
Mrs. Delanty, beginning to talk very fast; "if she
had followed me and Gus Fitz-Symons she mightn't
have been the last up."

The outer door of the kitchen here opened violently;
and Kate the General burst in with a foaming can of
milk in one hand, a lantern in the other, and a health-
ful countenance blazing with tidings.

"There's a gentleman after coming into the yard!"

she hissed. " I'd say it was the one was here last Sunday, and he leading a foxy horse, and it lame ! "

"Light the drawing-room fire!" commanded the widow, already on her feet. "It's Fanshawe ! If the horse is very bad he might have to stay for dinner ! "

"Merciful God!" interjected Kate, dashing the wisps of yellow hair out of her eyes.

"I'll give you word as soon as I can. There's a tin of soup—devil what's left of the beef—a sweet omelette—toasted cheese—don't open the soup till I give you word——!" She snatched the lantern out of Kate's red fist and was gone.

Miss Scanlan said nothing ; she had already caught up a paraffin can and a box of matches, and was away, like an incendiary, to the drawing-room.

As Mrs. Delanty faced once more the darkness and the cold wind of the yard she said to herself that if Mr. Fanshawe and his horse remained where she had last heard of them, at the bottom of the Kael, it would not have broken her heart. That he should have turned to her in his hour of need was, no doubt, gratifying, but she could have wished that the hour of need had not coincided with one of the few moments of real enjoyment that she had known that day.

The plight of the youth Fanshawe might indeed have moved to compassion a harder heart than that of the widow. The foxy horse was standing upon three legs, the fourth, of which only the toe touched the ground, was swaddled in rags. His suffering eye glinted white in the light of the lantern.

"Better get those dirty things off till we look at it," said Mrs. Delanty, authoritatively, putting the lantern on the ground.

Her practised fingers dealt speedily with the boot laces and the crooked pins by means of which the rags were kept *in situ*. The horse drooped his long nose over her, and touched her hair at intervals with his lips.

"No, I'll not hurt you, poor boy!" she said, accepting the warning, as she finally laid bare a jagged loose-lipped wound at the back of the white fetlock. "It's deep enough," she pronounced after a survey. "I suppose he did it getting out of the Kael. Those slatey stones in the bog-stuff are the mischief! I know enough of the Kael to keep clear of it when I can!"

"Well, if you ask me," said Fanshawe, in profound gloom, "I should say there wasn't a fence in this blessed country where he mightn't have done it. Anyhow, I noticed it first when I got him out of the Kael, if that's what you call the beastly place."

"It's not a fair place to ask a horse to jump," said Mrs. Delanty, "the Master and I took a different line altogether. Big jumping we had too—and there was no one but ourselves with them when he went to ground."

"A lot of people had to chuck it," said Fanshawe, "Miss Rowan, for one."

"So I heard," said the widow, eagerly.

"Pity too. She'd been going great guns up to that. I know I wish *I'd* chucked it. I had a dozen fellows dragging at the horse to get him out. He wouldn't even try. He just looked at 'em and said, 'Leave it to you, partner!' Sickening brute! Nothing but main strength and the ropes did it. We got him up to a farmhouse and they rubbed him down a bit and washed the cut."

"Washed!" interjected Mrs. Delanty, witheringly. "I wonder did they tell you when the rags were washed!"

"I believe the woman took them out of a hole in the wall of a cowhouse," said Fanshawe, vaguely.

"I wouldn't wonder!" said the widow.

"They were awfully decent anyhow. Jolly nice people, I call them. I got dried there, and they gave me a glass of whisky. My word! I tell you that *was* whisky! Old Clery was there; he said it was great stuff, it'd make a rabbit spit at a dog! I say, you do say funny things over here!"

"I daresay, between you and old Clery, there wasn't much left for the rabbit!" retorted the widow. "You'd say so anyhow by the way the bandages were put on!"

"Oh, help! Don't hit a man when he's down!" appealed Mr. Fanshawe, wholly out-classed, and aware of it; "you're my only hope! I thought I should have got him to the station, but it was getting worse all the time, and when I got to your gate I thought the only thing for it was to wire for the motor and throw myself on your mercy. I know you're a champion vet——" He looked at her humbly as he knelt beside her.

She glanced at him without replying, and Mr. Fanshawe said to himself that she was a little ripper.

Here Mrs. Delanty went to the house, and returned with bandages and bottles. She had also ordered the tin of soup to be opened.

Two hours later, Miss Scanlan, with a deep relief, found herself once more "below stairs" and in the comfortable society of Kate.

"Well, the omelette was grand," she said, tying a blue apron over her black best dress, "and you did first-rate in the parlour too!"

"Thank you, Miss," said poor Kate, whose face blazed like fire from mental stress as well as physical exertion. "Faith, I'm as tired this minute as if I was after walking to Cork with a bag o' male on me back!"

"You only made but the one mistake," continued Miss Janetta, "when you offered him the omelette and he having no plate in front of him!"

"Glory be to God! Didn't I feel the eye mistress put on me!" answered Kate with emotion. "When

a thing'd go wrong that way, an' I goin' round the
ladies and gentlemen, I'd busht out shweatin'!"

"Indeed *I* wouldn't blame you!" responded
Miss Janetta, sympathetically. "Here now," she
went on, "finish up the omelette yourself. You
didn't get your tea yet."

Some code of Kate's own sent her away into the
scullery, there, darkling, to devour the booty; Miss
Janette might be a fellow conspirator, but an instinct, which Kate could not have explained, decreed
that she should not eat in her presence. It was
known, as all things are known to servants, and
more especially to Irish servants, that Miss Janetta's
mother, that unhappy lady who had offered eighteen
pledges of affection to the Waterford butter merchant,
had come of what is spoken of, even in these days,
as "owld stock," and the fact was not forgotten.

The drawing-room bell rang, suddenly, angrily,
tossing itself head over heels on its spiral spring
under the ceiling.

"Mercy, Kate!" ejaculated Miss Janetta, "that's
for the coffee! And not a sign of a boil out of the
kettle!"

Her collaborator burst from the scullery like a
luggage train from a tunnel.

"Oh God!" she said, comprehensively, and with
entire reverence.

Upstairs in the drawing-room the lady of the
house sat in a mauve tea-gown, and smoked Fanshawe's cigarettes, and secretly found him rather a
bore, as much, at least, as any man could be a bore
to Mrs. Delanty. Her guest lay back in a tall grand-
father chair (Mrs. Delanty had successfully acquired
a *flair* for auctions and old furniture), looking, in his
muddy hunting clothes, like a Caldecott drawing,
and talked interminably of himself and his horses.
The spick and span little drawing-room was warm
and bright, the dinner, that gallant impromptu, had
imparted a mellow mood of well-being, the lamp

shed a pink and soothing glow upon all things, and
especially upon the soft, dark eyes and delicately cut
features of his little hostess. He was now luxuriously
giving her, in all its details, the history of the roan
horse he had bought from O'Callaghan—" Calligan "
he called him—of what he had said to O'Callaghan,
of what O'Callaghan had said to him. He had even
imparted to her the price he had paid to O'Callaghan.
Mrs. Delanty, who had long been acquainted with
the facts, was nevertheless gratified by the confidences.
She raised her pencilled eyebrows with a proper
surprise that O'Callaghan should have been so
worsted in the contest. She sweetly declined the
suggestion that she should come over and have a
ride on the road with the X.H. ; it was, she said,
her rule neither to borrow nor to lend a horse. " Poor
people could not afford to do these things," she
added, with a pathos that was not entirely assumed.

" Oh, but I wish you would, really," protested
Fanshawe, who was realizing more at each moment
what a nice little woman she was, and how pretty.
" I want to pass him on to my eldest brother, and
it would make all the difference if I could say he
was fit for his wife to ride."

Mrs. Delanty felt as if a window had been suddenly opened, and a chill wind had struck her in the
face. Any man was to her a possibility ; that was
the creed in which she and the Scanlan sisterhood
had been brought up, and when the possibility was
a tall and seemly youth, possessed of a motor
and three horses, and of a palpable admiration for
herself, she had, quite in the back of her mind, con-
structed a little cobweb palace in which she, a charming and fashionable spider, should reside in company
with this most eligible fly. The palace should be
in England, of course ; England was so much smarter
than Ireland.

" Oh, any horse will carry a lady," she said, while
the cobweb palace trembled in that same chill wind.

" Many a one I've got up on that never had so much
as a rug on him ! "

" Oh, but *you*—— ! " said Mr. Fanshawe, looking
at her with eyes that watered slightly, the result
partly of the wind, partly of the fire, and partly of
a sudden burst of affection, " *you* could ride anything ! That's what it is to have hands, you know
—such little hands, too ! "

Here Mr. Fanshawe adventurously laid hold of
Mrs. Delanty's wrist, and regarded the hand in
question with a fond, if not drivelling, smile.

Mrs. Delanty's prettily startled eyes looked into
his for a bewildering moment, and Fanshawe's
fingers trembled.

" No, no ! " said Mrs. Delanty, maternally, and
withdrew her hand.

" Oh, but I say—— " remonstrated her young
friend, looking ineffably silly, " mayn't I just look
at it ? "

" You may look at it as much as you like," returned
Mrs. Delanty, spreading her little claw in the air
like a starfish. It's not so small that you can't see
it from a respectable distance ! "

" You're very unkind to me ! " lamented Fanshawe.

" Don't cry ! " mocked the widow. " Little boys
can't have everything they want ! There now, I
believe I hear your motor coming for you this
minute."

" Oh, hang the motor ! " said Fanshawe, subsiding.

Mrs. Delanty swept her lashes upwards with a
laugh in her eye that told him she was not irrevocably
offended.

She had laid to heart one or two things in the
course of her career, and without being particularly
well acquainted with Byron, she had formed the
opinion that man's after-dinner love is of man's
life a thing apart, and also that to permit sporadic
demonstrations of this kind was a tactical error.

CHAPTER XIII

"THEY look tired enough, the creatures!" said Mrs. Fitz-Symons, standing in the middle kennel yard, with her hands on her hips, "there's some of them won't be fit to go out on Friday."

John Michael, seated on an upturned bucket with a hound between his knees, grunted repressively. No man likes to be told that his hounds are not fit to go out, least of all when he knows it himself.

" Look at old Governess and the way her eyes are back in her head! You'd say she was dying this minute!"

It was a sunny morning, and the hounds were lying like flies about the yard. One, presumably Governess, flopped a languid stern on the flags at the mention of her name, and one or two of the younger ones dragged themselves, yawning, on to their legs, and strolled to the railing between the yards to pay their respects to the visitor.

" They had as hard a day yesterday as they had this good while," said John Michael, pouring an evil-smelling decoction into the palm of his hand and proceeding to scrub it into his victim's shoulder. " This one hurt himself somehow coming down Moragh Hill, and a good few of them got thorns in their feet, but they'd do it again to-day if I asked them."

" Gus was greatly pleased with the way they behaved," said Mrs. Fitz-Symons, well aware that this gratifying fact was not likely to reach her younger son save through her, " and above all what delighted him was that he would be the one to cheer them when they marked the fox at the hole! Was it true what Tom Coyne tells me, that Lily Delanty

G

was with Gus every foot of the way ? and neither of
the pair of them ever jumped a fence at all ! "

Mrs. Fitz-Symons lowered her voice to the conspirator's pitch.

" How would I know ? " returned her son. " When-
ever I crossed a road they were on it before me.
When Jimmy Doyle and myself saw them before us
at the earth I declare we had to laugh ! "

" I hope in God Gus isn't taking a notion of her
again ! " said Mrs. Fitz-Symons, moving ponderously
round in order to see her son's face.

John Michael's hazel eyes met hers expressionlessly,
while his broad-topped fingers delicately explored
the hound's shoulder.

" He's torn the ligament," he said.

" Very well. I hope you'll like her when she's your
sister-in-law, and you and me are put out on the
roadside ! " exclaimed his mother, noting, even in
her wrath, how dark and curled were his long eyelashes, how smooth and clear the curve of his cheek.
" Well, Lily Delanty won't get *him* anyway ! " she
said to herself, with the intense possessiveness of a
mother in her eye as she looked at him, " not if she
was to put her eyes on sticks ! "

" She's so fond of the road she wouldn't give you
as much as the side of it itself ! " said John Michael,
with unwonted readiness.

Mrs. Fitz-Symons flung back her head and cackled
a quick appreciation of the jest. She laughed so loudly,
in fact, that the two puppies of her latest rearing
raised their heads and smiled sympathetically.
" Well done, Johnny ! I declare I'd give a pound
to tell her you said that ! Look at my darling
Buxom and Bluemaid, and they laughing too ! "

" I wonder they're not too tired," said her son.

" Well, if I was on my dying bed I'd have to laugh
at that ! " said his proud mother.

Something like a coach-horn, blown with extraordinary sonority, sounded from afar.

"That's Mr. Fanshawe's motor," remarked John
Michael. "He was over to Mrs. Delanty's this
morning to look at his horse."

His mother immediately bundled out of the yard
to a point of observation, and the motor boomed
and buzzed past, with a renewed extravaganza in
her honour.

"Well, that beats all!" she said, returning to the
yard, where the hounds, who had started to attention,
were sulkily resuming their slumbers. "Talk of
an angel, indeed! Who do you think was with
Fanshawe in it, only me lady Delanty! Listen to
them now!" as a clarion call, already half a mile
away, proclaimed the progress of the party through
the country. "And if you'll believe me, she had
that poor old Janetta stuck up all alone in the back
seat! You'd pity the creature, she looked so frightened! She has her there for propriety, I suppose.
Well, well, well! Thank God, no one's asking *me*
to go in a motor, and what's more, I wouldn't go
if they did, for I haven't so much as put my nose
into the kitchen this blessed morning!"

"Mary Anne will have your life," remarked John
Michael, rising to his feet.

"She's welcome to it!" retorted his mother,
"I'd sooner go without my dinner any day than be
bothered ordering it! But that wouldn't do for
Gus!"

"Well, you needn't order lunch for me anyhow.
I'm going away over the hill to see did they open the
holes in the Lake View covert last night."

Mrs. Fitz-Symons' blue eyes brightened.

"Sure, they'd give you a bit of luncheon there,"
she said, quickly. "I don't like your going without
your meals this way, my doatie boy."

"I'll not go to Lake View House, if that's what
you mean," answered John Michael, with equal speed;
looking both stubborn and frightened.

Faintly, across the fields, from a new and

unexpected point of the compass, came the blatant chant of the " Gabriel-horn."

Mrs. Fitz-Symons and her son regarded one another in complete stillness.

" It's up at the house," breathed Mrs. Fitz-Symons fatefully.

" Well, I'm off," said John Michael, with the iron determination that even the weakest of men can show in such an emergency.

Mrs. Fitz-Symons uttered a groan like a horse on its deathbed. " Go to Lake View ! " she called after him.

His way took him south, with the sun in his face, and the light wind followed him. So also did the two white wire-haired kennel terriers, Dhoosh and Sue, serious, like their master, and like him possessed of souls given singly to the chase. He went up through steep fields, where his step-brother's cattle were grazing desultorily among clumps of furze and rusty bracken ; he would tell Gus he thought that it'd be as good for them to be inside as to be walking the flesh off their bones for the sake of what grass they could pick off the bare ground. He went higher, and the rocks came shouldering up through the thin soil, and the grass was yellow and coarse, and the furze grew low and thick in many a place where he himself had put a match to it in the year that was past. There was a cold warble of water somewhere near, and soon he stepped across a hill-stream, hidden in a deep channel under briars on which a tawny leaf or two still hung. He heard the dogs splashing in its depths, gathering information about water-rats; and he kicked a stone down through the tangle, just to provide them with a sensation. A short distance ahead of him a couple of snipe shot up from a damp patch, uttering their dry, rasping cry, and fled down the wind, soaring and diving in sickle swoops. John Michael brought his stick to his shoulder, following them with it against the pale

blue sky, and said to himself that he wished he had
thought to bring the gun out of the kennels with
him. The dogs, who had burst out of the stream
at the sound, looked at him questioningly.

" Was it a rat ? " they said ; " my father, shall
we smite them ? "

John Michael laughed at them.

" You know well," he told them, " if I'd had a
shot at those lads the pair of you would have been
half-way home by now ! "

Dhoosh and Sue were gun-shy, a fact which they
desperately endeavoured to conceal.

John Michael went on his way, walking lightly and
fast up the broken ground. He passed without a
glance a ring of rough stones set upright round a
level place on the hill-side, like a group of grey
women ; humble, unlovely, witnesses to a forgotten
worship and a dim, half-forgotten race. He spoke
of them, as every one else did, as the Standing
Stones ; he could have told you of three or four
other circles like this one, and he would have added
that often he had picked up the drag of a fox just
hereabouts. It certainly would not have occurred
to him that he had anything in common with
those past and primitive hunters who had set them
up.

A little further on were the broken walls of a
roofless cottage (" a cowlach " John Michael called it)
and he straightway thought of the stoat whom, more
than once, he had seen dodging about it. The ground
lay in hummocks and ridges, like an old graveyard ;
he was walking over what had been the potato plot
of the cottage, where the potatoes had melted to
black slime in the days of the Famine. It was
grown over now with heather and bracken, and where
the door of the cottage had been was an entangle-
ment of briars, strong as barbed wire. The dogs
were yelping in the nettles and briars inside the walls.
Decidedly the stoat was in it.

"They'll not stir him!" thought John Michael.
" A pity they wouldn't get him in the open!"

He had not the heart to call them out of it, and
he stood for a moment and listened.   Something
went in little jumps through the heather above the
cottage ; his eye, quick as a cat's, caught the whisk
of a tiny black tail, like the tail of a fairy horse.

"Hulla! Hulla! Urrish! Sue! Urrish! Dhoosh!"
yelled John Michael, as many a bare-legged hunter
before him had yelled on that hill-side.

Dhoosh and Sue responded with the shrieks of
souls in torment.   The stoat's bolt-hole was too small
for them ; two agonised white faces showed for a
second at the top of the wall of the cowlach and
fell back again.   John Michael uttered another
pre-historic howl, and, as if lifted by its inspiration,
they were on the top of the wall and down into the
heather on the other side.   The chase was a hot one,
and Dhoosh and Sue and John Michael made as
much noise over it as if they were two packs of
foxhounds.   At intervals, between the bunches of
heather and furze-bushes, he saw the stoat, going
at that peculiar frisky gallop that seems so casual
and is so very much to the point, and on these occasions the screeches that he gave vent to were highly
creditable to his wind and condition, considering that
he was running up hill and keeping on very fair terms
with the dogs.   At one point they had a long check,
during which John Michael thrashed the furze bushes,
and the dogs, completely off their heads, as is the
wont of terriers, went with frog-springs, and kangaroo-
bounds, through the heather, hoarsely panting with
indignation, pausing only to flap their torn ears, and
to stare at John Michael in a frenzy of questioning.

Neither Dhoosh nor Sue had, it is hardly necessary
to say, the smallest desire to eat the stoat, nor would
it have occurred to John Michael to say that he was
righteously engaged in the destruction of vermin ;
he and the terriers were in the grip of an identical

passion, the passion of the Chase, that had swayed
the men of these hills since before the beginning of
time. The ragged outline of an old wall was sil-
houetted against the sky along the crest of the
hill.

"I'll cast them on there," he thought, "it's there
he's gone! Hulla! Try forrad, Dhoosh! Try forrad,
Sue, good dogs!"

He sprinted up the hill; not a kern of a score of
centuries back would have tackled it in better style.
The dogs raced with him, their heads up; they knew
that if sport were to be had he would show it to
them. On the crisp turf along the ridge of the hill
they picked up the line again, but the wall beat them;
and somewhere down in its ancient foundations the
stoat heard them, and laughed in its impish heart.

CHAPTER XIV

THE baffled squeals of Dhoosh and Sue were
heard also, but by quite another person, who
was seated with her back to a rock, a little lower
down on the southern side of the hill. The squeals
were, for some time, mingled in the ears of this
person with the measured accents of a voice that
was reading aloud, the voice of Ulick Adare, who
was reading to Katharine with the seriousness that no
author, however keen may be his sense of humour,
is able to withhold from his own handiwork. Katharine had, up to this point, been a perfectly satisfactory
audience. The sentences winged their way, like
birds of strong flight, they took her with them away
into the world of ideas. Fragments of the poetry
he was criticizing came in, and stirred her like
music.

"One in whose gentle bosom I
　　Could tell my inmost heart of woes,
　Like the care-burthened honey-fly
　　That hides his murmurs in the rose."

The metaphor gathered to its close and fell like a
dew-drop ; he was silent for a moment, and she was
silent too, just as he would have wished her to be.
He went on reading, and at intervals she murmured
appreciation ; she sat upright, and glowed at him in
full-hearted enthusiasm, she told him, with eyes of the
clearest and greyest sincerity, that she had always
felt the things that he had said, but had never known
how to say them. She was at all times direct in her
methods, and he, who had often explained to her the
superior attractiveness of suggestion and subtlety,
met her honest eyes with a catch of the heart, and
thought that last summer had come again.

In the shelter of the rock, with the midday sun full
on them, it was indeed as warm as summer. The
hill, pale yellow and brown, flowed down below them
to the dark firwood behind the house. The smoke
from the chimneys spired bluely up in the tranquil
air ; bluer than it, and many times bluer than the
pale sky, the lake lay like a patch of a peacock's breast
in a setting of gold, where the dead reeds held the sun.
The leisurely rattle of a cart came up from the grey
road, and beside the lake a ploughman was calling to
his horses. The seagulls that stooped and clustered
in the wake of the plough looked like white butterflies.
At the end of a sentence Adare looked at her for an
instant, and with that lost his place, and laughed, and
said, " I'm dazzled by the sun in your hair ! "

Katharine did not hear him, she had turned her head
aside, and was listening to another voice, voices
rather.

" I'm sorry," she said, " I didn't catch that last
sentence."

" Oh, it was nothing——"

When a shy heart speaks—and Ulick Adare had the

shy heart that is born of the sense of humour—it cannot utter itself twice.

"There it is again! Don't you hear it? As if a dog were being hurt—— "

She started to her feet. Round the end of the rock came a spying face, and looked at them, the white face of Sue, with, as it were, a red handkerchief wrapped round it.

"Oh, it's covered with blood!" cried Katharine, in horror. "It's throat has been cut!"

Ulick Adare glanced at Sue under the peak of his cap, and said, with a want of sympathy that under the circumstances was pardonable—

"It has torn its ears in the briars. The audience can keep their seats."

He too had kept terriers, and had hunted rabbits, long ago, in the County Wicklow.

"How odious you are!" said Katharine, kneeling down and delicately examining the torn tan ears. "I believe it's Mr. Fitz-Symons' Sue."

At her name the lady in question immediately flung herself on her side and languished sycophantically.

"Here's her owner," said Ulick Adare in a voice that bristled. "H'are you, Fitz-Symons?"

"Good morning," replied John Michael, standing amazed and snatching off his cap. "Ah, don't touch her, Miss Rowan, she'll destroy your gloves."

He was standing above her, and his face had for background that most beautiful of all backgrounds, the blue deeps of the sky; the chase of the stoat had kindled his eyes and warmed the clear brown of his skin. Katharine looked up at him, and finding that a quite unexpected colour rose into her face, looked down at Sue again. Adare saw the inexplicable blush, and his heart stood still and cold for an instant, and then sprang forward again with a dizzy and wholly conventional desire to take John Michael by his brown throat and pitch him into the lake.

Katharine, angrily reasoning with herself as to the cause of the blush, decided that it was the result partly of surprise, and partly because Ulick Adare's indignation was so palpable that she was ashamed of it.

Had Mr. Adare been a shade less dizzy he might possibly have perceived the interrupter's acute sense of his own superfluity.

"I was just going to have a look at the earths below," apologised John Michael.

There was a pause, during which Katharine communed with herself as to whether it would be inhuman not to ask him to luncheon ; she had remained on her knees, because to stand up seemed over-polite, and to sit down again beside Ulick Adare had, in some absurd way, become impossible. Here Sue suddenly and abundantly licked the nose of her sympathizer.

"Down, Sue !" said John Michael. "I hope your horse is all right after the hunt ? " he went on, not because he wanted to make conversation, but because he was sincerely interested in the matter.

Katharine started to her feet.

"I'm not quite happy about one of his fore-legs," she began very seriously. "It was rather swelled this morning."

Ulick Adare got up and crammed his manuscript into his pocket, and wondered how much of her interest in it had been genuine. This was the real thing, at all events, he thought, fuming to himself.

"Did he put bandages on him last night ? " asked John Michael. "I wouldn't mind his legs filling a bit after a hard day. He never had a doing like that before."

"Oh, if I could only have got him over the Kael ! " cried Katharine, effusively. "Your delightful mare simply floated over it like—like a swallow ! That's a brilliantly original simile ! " she added self-consciously, with a side-glance at Ulick Adare. She had an agreeable side-long look, that was both rallying and friendly, but Adare remained blankly unresponsive. "I had never ridden a run before. It was quite wonderful! One crowded hour of glorious life!"—she rhapsodized, and looked again at the man who could understand her.

It was the man who did not understand her who replied:

"It was more than an hour," said John Michael. "I made it an hour and seventeen minutes."

Ulick Adare met her look for the first time, with eyes so deliberately remote as to leave her in no doubt whatever as to his inner satisfaction.

"'The little more and how much it is!'" he murmured to the elements.

Katharine turned her back on him.

"I wonder if you would be so very kind as to come and look at the foreleg?" she said to John Michael, with profound deference. "I've no one to give me advice!"

She had divined the one possible snare, and it did not fail.

"Well, I'd like to have a look at him," admitted John Michael, truthfully.

They walked down the hill by a steep and wandering path. Adare stalked in front, as far, at least, as was consistent with the nature of the ground. He wore an air of complete detachment from the party; he whistled, thinly, a fragment of highly modern music, an errant and perverse motive that the flutes of the Queen's Hall had piped to him and to her not long since, and Katharine recognized it, as it was perhaps intended that she should. She felt again the thick red carpet under her feet, and heard the gentle breathing of Jean Masterman, in furtive slumber, beside her; she remembered the cold fog in Langham Place.

Ulick Adare made a mistake in whistling that tune. She turned to John Michael, following in her track as silently as the dogs in his, but without their enjoyment.

"How delicious the air is here! And the colour, and the silence! Don't you wish we were hunting?"

"I'm afraid there wouldn't be much of a scent," replied John Michael, with unshaken practicality; "it was hardly the terriers could acknowledge that weasel above on the hill."

With which Katharine laughed in frank, if effete, enjoyment. She was in the mood to feel the charm of simplicity, and to think that the Men of Action were worthier in their generation than the Men of Words.

And, after all (to Mrs. Fitz-Symons' subsequent exultation), John Michael had to partake of luncheon with the ladies of Lake View. There was no way out of it for him. He had surveyed Dermot, had given a well considered opinion on the foreleg under suspicion (to the effect that the horse had boxed it with the other foot), and was spreading his pinions for flight, when the parlourmaid picked her way delicately into the stable with the information that lunch was on the table and that Mrs. Masterman hoped they would come in at once. He had neither the nerve nor the ingenuity demanded by such an extremity, and presently found himself seated at the luncheon-table, in awful proximity to the French governess, and confronted with the position of guest-in-chief.

The position of guest, whether chief or otherwise, was one to which John Michael was entirely unaccustomed, and it cannot be said that he rose to the occasion. Had he desired to show the length and thickness of the black eyelashes so much admired by his mother, he could hardly have kept his eyes more persistently upon his plate. He ate everything that was offered to him, bolting all with the speed of one of his own hounds, not because he was greedy but because he was frightened; for the same reason he submissively swallowed glasses of claret, a drink which he abhorred, and was wont, in happier moments, to describe as "th' image of ink."

Mrs. Masterman felt sorry for him ; she was always ready to be sorry for a man, but she said to herself that if Katharine chose to import such a being she must take the consequences. She was not altogether pleased with Katharine in the matter of the Being, and thought it not inadvisable that she should suffer. Moreover, she had to supervise the stoking of her offspring, and, in common with many mothers, at the Children's Dinner she subordinated her social instincts to those of the female beast of prey, whose single desire it is to give to her young their meat in due season.

It is perhaps unnecessary to say that Mr. Adare was displeased with Miss Rowan ; he demonstrated the fact, after his kind, by a cool and equable silence, and by a slight unreadiness of attention on those occasions when, monologue and catechism having alike exhausted themselves in vain upon John Michael, she turned to him for help.

He did indeed converse from time to time with Mademoiselle, in her own language, an attention which Katharine felt to be a studied act of ill-breeding. He ate nothing, a fact not lost upon his cousin Jean, as being a recognised signal of displeasure on his part ; his conduct was irreproachable and thoroughly disagreeable. The coffee and the cigarettes did nothing for the situation. John Michael did not smoke ; he was secretly amazed at seeing his much-feared hostess do so. He thought it was only Mrs. Delanty and " the like of her " who did it, " to show off," and he noted with approval that Miss Rowan pushed the box on to him without taking one.

" I daren't do anything to damage my nerve !" she apologised. " What ! you afraid too ? "

" I wouldn't like it," said John Michael, uncomfortably, and wondering how much longer this purgatory was going to last. As if in answer to prayer came a muffled and heavy knocking at one of the windows, followed by an apologetic cough, and

a bearded countenance presented itself at the
glass.

"Another beggar!" said Mrs. Masterman, "that's
the third to-day!"

Following on the cough came a sound as of someone tearing the ivy from the walls of the house. Mrs.
Masterman rose indignantly.

"Really—— " she began.

"That's not a beggar," said John Michael, rising
quickly from his place: "that's James Hefferman
of Killeenascreena. I think he has a horse with him;
I see the end of a halter in his hand. I believe it's
me he's looking for. Maybe I'd better go out to
him."

The door closed behind Mr. Fitz-Symons.

"Exit Dumb Crambo!" said Ulick Adare. "If
his conversation were in the same class with his
appetite he would be the life and soul of any party!"

CHAPTER XV

AS Katharine hurried into a coat and cap in
the hall she called out to the dining-room
in general that she was going out to see the fun, and
added, not without defiance, that she supposed they
were too lazy to come.

"Not too lazy," replied the voice of Jean Masterman," but too entirely sensible to do what bores us."

Miss Rowan proceeded to the yard, where the first
stage of the enquiry into the merits of James Hefferman's mare was already in progress. A small and
tattered saddle lay on the ground, and the eyes of
John Michael met hers over the mare's withers on
which his chin was laid. They were oblivious of her
presence.

"Measure her any way in the world," remarked the mare's proprietor to the universe, "she's on the brink of sixteen hands, and she'll make the sixteen before she's done."

John Michael went on with his examination in silence, and James Hefferman continued his address, taking Katharine as its focal point.

"I wouldn't be for selling her at all, but I have no place for the likes of her. If a hundred acres was before her it wouldn't be enough for her. And as for fences——" he paused, and again addressed the universe. "Oh, Christians! Whatever she could face at she could jump it!"

He had a long narrow face, like a sour old dachshund's, with a decent fringe of grey whisker; his eyes dwelt upon Katharine with melancholy solemnity.

The mare had a thick, iron-grey fleece, and a long tail with a white end to it, like the tag on a fox's brush. She looked down with a shy and kindly eye at John Michael, who was thoughtfully handling one of her fetlocks.

"Is she quiet?" asked Katharine, respectfully.

"Is it quiet? By the gash of war! you could pull the leg out of her and she'd not mind!"

"Pick up her foreleg," said John Michael, running a quiet hand over one of the mare's hocks.

"There's no occasion, Master Johnny. She'll not rise a heel to you. Sure the lads does be pulling hairs out of her tail for their fish-hooks, and she'd not say a word to them."

Katharine watched John Michael, and yearned exceedingly to know the hundredth part of what he knew about a horse, and wondered incidentally how he contrived to make his shabby home-spun coat to look as if it were well cut. Tim, who was by this time deep in the affair, was now engaged in running the mare up and down the yard, to her intense and wholly reasonable surprise.

" She is a proud grand mare indeed, and carries herself very lovely ! " pronounced her owner. " Throw the saddle on her, Tim. What signifies parading her this way. Get on her back, Master Johnny, and ride her away in the field. When she begins to gallop you'd lose your senses."

" Wait awhile till I put *our* saddle on her, sir," said Tim, eagerly.

There were two fields near the house, large agreeable fields, and to them Katharine, Tim, and James Hefferman presently hurried side by side in the wake of the grey mare. She moved at a placid and springy walk, regarding her surroundings with profound interest, but without excitement. It was past three o'clock, and the sun was getting low. The brown hill held purple shadows in its folds ; there was a haze over the fields, and a flush in the western sky that hinted at a coming frost. Dhoosh and Sue, who had borne the tedium of the proceedings in the yard with a frigid composure acquired in many such scenes, strayed away to a briary fence that bordered on the road, and there pursued tepid investigations in ancient trails, much as one might read an old newspaper in a waiting-room.

The mare and John Michael paced round the field with an equal sobriety. One of the things that Katharine found attractive about John Michael was his seriousness. She explained to herself that he had none of the second-rate desire to be facetious ; in fact, he was not second rate, he was merely provincial, quite a different thing, though Jean Masterman had refused to see the difference where he was concerned. The object of these reflections here drove his heels into the woolly sides of the mare. A long, slouching trot was the response. Another kick, and she flung herself forward into a canter—a big, active canter, clumsy, but enthusiastic.

" Ah, ha ! That's the way ! " shouted her owner as she swept past. " Try her with a lep now ! " It seemed to Katharine that John Michael was doing nothing special, yet the mare at every stride went better and more collectedly ; as she neared the bank at the end of the field her head went up and she pricked her ears.

James Hefferman caught Katharine by the arm. "Look at her now ! ' Forgive any horse that'll cock his ears ! '—that's what the people say. Look at her, look at her ! "

The mare jumped on to the bank with a will, and, with a flourish of her long tail, was away into the next field. The audience could no longer see her, but they could hear the rhythmic beat of her hoofs and the slaps of John Michael's ash-plant as he set her going to try her wind.

" I had a lovely colt one time from that one's dam," remarked James Hefferman, " the grandest one ever I bred. Sure I thought the world wasn't good enough for him. And I put him within in the best house I had. Sun, moon, nor stars didn't shine on him, nor the breath of Heaven didn't touch him ; and after all he died on me ! I wouldn't have wished it for twenty pounds."

" You would not indeed, sir," said Tim, sympathetically.

" Well, that's the way always," resumed James Hefferman, in philosophic acceptance of the mysterious decrees of providence. " And look now at this one, that I didn't lave hand nor foot to, only to throw her out on the hill with the bullockeens, she's as healthy as a stone."

Here the narrative ceased, as the grey face and pricked ears of the neglected one rose into sight above the line of the fence. Up came the clever forefeet, planted one on either side of a stone that lay on the top of the bank ; up came the hind feet with an equal precision, and Katharine's 'prentice heart leaped with her as she leaped out into the field ; and still John Michael seemed to Katharine to be

H

doing nothing beyond sitting lithely on the mare's
back. He thundered past, the mare's mane and tail
flying gallantly and classically out. His cap had
fallen off, and his hair was rough on his forehead.
In the lowered rays of the sun his boyish head and
light figure were set in a dazzling halo ; the two
men watched him with narrowed eyes and wrinkled
noses and open mouths, after the singularly hideous
manner of their kind. Katharine, with an enthusiasm that she would, not long ago, have been the first
to denounce as gush, strung together phrases about
Grace and Courage and Speed, while James Hefferman
with an equal enthusiasm and a swifter method,
turned to Tim and said ardently :

" Ye'd say he was sewn to the saddle ! "

John Michael rode back out of the evening glow
and the halo.

" She's a nice mare," he said, as he slipped off her
back. " She gives you a good feel, but she's green
still."

" Well for as green as she is, Master Johnny,"
trumpeted James Hefferman, " there isn't a fence on
my land but she has it lepped. There's one of my little
gerrls is riding her bare-backed every day round the
place ! "

" Will I run for the saddle, Miss ? " said Tim,
tracking unerringly the processes of thought in
Katharine's mind, " and let yourself try her ? She'd
carry you to fortune ! "

John Michael was intently engaged in listening to
the mare's breathing. Katharine looked waveringly
at Tim.

" Arrah, why not ! " said James Hefferman.

Miss Rowan stole up to her room by the back
stairs. This was not a matter in which Jean Masterman would sympathize, and discussions were a bore.
In five minutes she emerged with a habit skirt on and,
by what she felt to be singular ill-fortune, ran right
into Ulick Adare in the stable yard.

" What are you going to do now ? " he said, looking at her attire with much disfavour.

" I'm going to try that mare," said Katharine
defiantly.

" You're going to ride that woolly beast ? " he
said, with what seemed to her quite unwarrantable
indignation. " Why can't Fitz-Symons ride her
for himself ? Does he want to stick some one with
her as a lady's hack ? "

" I ride her because I choose to do so," said Katharine, magnificently, hobbling away as fast as her
safety-skirt would permit.

" Of course that's an entirely logical reason ! " he
retorted.

" It's good enough for me ! " said Katharine in
a blaze, and plunged into the muddy lane that led
to the field.

By the time she had got to the end of the lane
she and her wrath were far enough apart for the
reflection to intervene that often as she had wrangled
with Ulick Adare this was the first time that they
had lost their tempers with each other. It was a
regrettable incident, but he had begun it.

When she rejoined the party in the field her saddle
was on the mare.

" She's a bit strong in the mouth," said John
Michael, regarding Katharine rather dubiously,
" but she's as quiet as a sheep. Trot her a bit before
you canter her. I think it'd be as well for you not
to try jumping her."

" Ha ! Ha ! I'll go bail that much wouldn't
surpass her Ladyship ! " cried James Hefferman.

" Hold your tongue, you fool ! " said John Michael,
in an aside that Katharine did not hear.

The mare accepted the presence of a petticoat
upon her back with a placidity that spoke well for her
friendship with James Hefferman's daughter.
When she trotted, Katharine felt as if she were
sitting on the bows of a big boat in a rough sea;

when she cantered, which she did with entire amia-
bility, it felt like riding over a succession of fences.
How had John Michael appeared to sit upon her
with the swaying ease that implies comfort ?   How,
also, had he turned and twisted her like a polo-pony ?
Her nose was set for the fence at the end of the field,
and it was as much as her present rider could do to
turn her from it.   She did so, however, and continued
the circuit of the field, aware by this time that as long
as the grey mare wished to canter she would find
it necessary to fall in with her wishes.   On the left
was the briary fence, beyond it the empty road.
A large humming sound became audible behind her,
the sound of a motor, and Katharine snatched a
shorter hold of the clumsy reins.   It came on in
swift crescendo, and culminated in a fantasia of
unearthly music as the motor whizzed past.   The
mare gave a ponderous swerve, mixed up with a
buck, a complicated manœuvre, in the course of
which she contrived to cross her forelegs.   Katharine felt the rough grey mane in her face, and
then the ground seemed to fly up to meet her,
and she was aware of some vast, yet remote, shock of
impact.

It was not at all unpleasant.   This Katharine explained over and over again in a dark place, where
people were talking far away in midget voices and
there was a pulse in the darkness.   An epoch of some
kind occurred, a long epoch, and the place was less
dark.   Something under her cheek was harsh and
uncomfortable ;   it was drab and annoying, with a
herring-bone pattern in it, and a watch was ticking
loudly quite near.   With a great effort she opened
her eyes ;   something was between her and the sky,
something that at first presented itself in the form of
spinning concentric circles of azure blue, and black,
and orange.   It steadied down gradually, and presently
became the face of Ulick Adare.   Katharine gazed up
at it, and said very clearly and slowly :

" How much the mental consciousness is in advance of the physical ! "

Then she heard Jean Masterman give a shaky laugh and say:

" There's the authentic Katharine, anyhow ! "

The next thing that struck her was the fact that Ulick Adare was in his shirt-sleeves.

" Where's your coat ? " she said.

" Under you. Never mind. Drink this."

He slid one hand gently under her shoulders and raised her a little.

Brandy and water out of a kitchen cup is a nauseous beverage, but she swallowed it obediently and felt better. Like a mountain behind her was the consciousness of the unknown something that had taken place.

" What has happened to me ? " she said, looking with an effort from one face to another. " Am I hurt ? "

" No, dearest," said Jean. " I think you're all right. You've had a fall."

This fact seemed too large for Katharine's apprehension ; she closed her eyes again and felt very tired.

" Feel her pulse, Johnny," said the practical Mrs. Delanty. " He's half a doctor, you know ! " she added.

Katharine was aware of two icy fingers and a thumb upon her wrist ; the arm that was still supporting her shoulder stiffened.

" I'd say the pulse was good," said John Michael modestly. " She fell on her head. It's just a touch of concussion, I expect."

" Let me stand up," said Katharine. " I'm really all right."

Adare lifted her smoothly and steadily, but she felt as if she were made of lead.

" I didn't think you were so strong ! " she said to him, with the intention of being polite, while the field and the fences rocked nauseatingly ; she leaned against him and saw them all, Mrs. Delanty, Fanshawe, Jean Masterman, John Michael, and, a little way off, James Hefferman and Tim, standing by the grey mare, all of them with their eyes fixed upon her.

A certain historic " Punch " picture flashed into her mind.

" And there be t'owd mare, and she be stearin' too, surely ! " she said, and laughed feebly.

" Oh, *you're* all right ! " said Jean, in a jovial voice with a break in it.

With which Katharine for no reason that she knew of, laid her head on the thing nearest to her, which happened to be Ulick Adare's shoulder, and there wept.

CHAPTER XVI

FOLLOWING on this came a night and a day, during which Katharine galloped round and round the grass field on the grey mare, always with the same growing stress, always ending with the same blind shock and obliteration, while the four notes of the motor trumpet reiterated themselves in a continuous chant. Headache was in and through the hours, and stiffness, as of all enveloping lumbago.

" Ah, she had a point or two of temperature," said the dispensary doctor, easily. " That'd keep her a bit fidgety." He added that all she need do was to stay in bed and keep warm, that the frost was the hardest he had seen for ten years, that he wouldn't come again without they'd send for him, he was tiring two horses a day as it was ; and finally, that he thought the young lady had the best of it, in bed in this cruel weather.

No one in their senses has ever been deceived by
consolations such as these.   Bed is in itself a slavery,
almost an illness, and those who are walking about
in the world, even the chilliest world, are a different
and a free race.   Katharine stayed in bed with the
shutters shut, and Mrs. Masterman conscientiously
refrained from telling her anything that would interest
her.   It was through Caroline, the housemaid, who
had heard it from Tim, that she learned that Mr.
Fitz-Symons had bought the grey mare, and Caroline
(whose sister, it may be remembered, had driven in
chariot-races at Olympia) had added that Tim had
said that Mr. Fitz-Symons had knocked five pounds
off her price because she had crossed her legs when
she fell with Miss Rowan.   " That *was* a set-out,
Miss ! " Caroline had ended, summing up the disaster
sympathetically.

This instance of John Michael's practicality was
not perhaps quite what Katharine could have
wished.   The ideal hero would have bought the horse
at any cost and shot it dead on the spot.   The point,
however, was, to what extent could John Michael
be considered the hero.   As she lay there, idle and
dreamy, and seeing things a little out of proportion,
after the manner of people who lie in bed, she saw
him in many aspects, always, like Saint George, on
horseback.   She saw him galloping down into the
frosty sunset ; she saw him in his red coat against
the grey sky, on the ridge of the hill, with his hounds
about his horse's feet ; she saw him riding at the
Kael on the chestnut mare, and knew what was the
quality in him that lifted her over it.   She could
feel herself charging it on Dermot, and her heart
beat harder and harder ;   Dermot always jumped
it in these visions, and John Michael and she, alone
with the hounds, went on and on illimitably.   She
arranged with herself during those twilight days that
the first and the last word in life was physical courage.
It might not be the greatest quality, it was certainly

the most attractive, the most desired ; the redeem-
ing quality, with the alchemy in it that turns base
metals into gold.   For her, at this particular juncture,
courage found its best expression in horsemanship,
and horsemanship was summed up in John Michael.
It meant so much besides courage, she told herself ;
sympathy, and determination, and patience, and
tact, and all these fused and glowing in the white
light of danger.   " Noble horsemanship," Shake-
speare called it, recognizing in it some fine output
of soul.

Here the thought of John Michael's horrified
amazement at finding himself attired in these attributes, felled her and her phrases at a stroke.   They
would have scandalized his simplicity, she thought,
that other great quality that she had discovered in
him.

" Simplicity and Courage ! " she summarized, her
head beginning to ache, " as far as mere character
goes, what more is wanted ? "

The last evening of her captivity came, and she
was sitting by her bedroom fire when Jean Masterman came up to smoke her after dinner cigarette
with the invalid, as was her custom.

" I hope you ate your snipe, my dear ? " she said,
sitting down and battering the fire into a blaze.
" Vile coal this is ! Parkington says that Tim assures
her that it is well known that the English fill the
coal ships with stones for the Irish market ! I really
think he's right.   Tweetie Pupsy !   Yes !   Here's
your coffee ! "

This to her small and effete red " Pom," who addressed himself with tiny and cat-like lappings to
the saucer that she set down for him.   " I may tell
you," she went on, " that Parkington is in love with
Tim ! "

" Parkington ! " exclaimed Katharine, " why, he
can only just read and write, and he's half her age ! "

" That's part of his attraction, I suppose, and I've

no doubt he's far more agreeable than the men of
her own class that she meets in England. I shouldn't
be in the least surprised if the old idiot ended by
marrying him." Mrs. Masterman put her feet on
the fender. "You never told me if you liked the
snipe. Ulick says the country is over-run with
poachers like himself, and he had to walk miles
for it."

Katharine made a suitable acknowledgment.

"William always says Ulick is as pretty a snipe-
shot as he's ever seen," remarked Mrs. Masterman,
falling into the flagrant error of praising, where a
higher diplomacy would have counselled slight and
stimulating disparagement. "Woodcock, too, for
the matter of that. It does seem a pity that he can't
afford to live at his own place."

"I think he prefers London," said Katharine.
"He and his friends can sit there in their club,
saying brilliant things to each other all day. That's
what they really enjoy!"

"My dear, he *must* live in London, for his work,
he would lose touch if he did not," expostulated Mrs.
Masterman.

"It's not a man's life," said Katharine, senten-
tiously, "eating late suppers and polishing phrases!"

"It's a case of ' no song, no supper,' late or otherwise!" retorted Mr. Adare's cousin, preparing a lap
for the Pom, who floated into it as lightly as thistle-
down, "if he didn't polish his phrases he would have
to polish empty plates! And so would his mother.
That's how he keeps her and the place going, poor
wretch! And such a nice old place! And an awful
peacock there too! Wasn't there, my little thing-
thing?" she added, confidentially, to the Pom, who
looked at her with eyes like wet boot-buttons, and
coiled herself for sleep.

"Jean, please don't drivel to that little brute,"
said Katharine, with the irritability proper to the
convalescent.

There was a silence.

" Dumb Crambo came over with his mamma to enquire for you," resumed Mrs. Masterman with dangerous sweetness. " Without mamma he would not again have ventured to put his nose inside the door ! "

" I don't know who you are talking about," said Miss Rowan, coldly.

" It was of the nature of a visit of apology," continued Jean, treating the remark with the contempt which it indeed deserved. " Mrs. Fitz-Symons said that if Johnny had thought the dirty motor was within a mule's screech of the place he'd never have let Miss Rowan up on the horse. Johnny, you will be surprised to hear, said nothing, but he wriggled very sympathetically."

" I fail to see why any one need apologize in the matter," said Katharine, from the back of her highest horse. " I think that at my age I might be considered competent to judge for myself."

" Mrs. Fitz-Symons is not of your opinion, and no more is your friend the Master. Judging by what the Widow Delanty tells me, he seems to have dealt very faithfully with Dumb Crambo in the matter."

" Don't you think that rather moderate jest has had its day ? " said Katharine, coming out into the open, as her tormentor had desired. " I cannot imagine why you and Mr. Adare take up this position of despising Mr. Fitz-Symons. I call it very bad form. Of course his limitations are obvious, but they are not his fault, and he is incapable of doing or saying anything ungentlemanlike. For my part——" Here Miss Rowan sat erect upon her sofa, " I like him and I respect him ! " Her face burned, and when she picked up a paper with which to screen it from the fire, her hand was shaking.

Jean looked quickly at her, and then laughed, in her pleasant, leisurely way.

" Really I am very much to be pitied ! First
Parkington, and now you ! But my sympathies
are with Parkington ; as far as agreeability goes,
my money's on Tim ! "

Katharine was very angry.

" If you're going to class me with Parkington . . ."
she began.

Jean leaned forward and laid her hand upon
Katharine's knee. Her hand was white and capable,
and instinct with the maternal quality that was in her.

" You silly old thing ! " she said, caressingly, " of
course, I don't put you in the same class as Parkington ! Parkington's the best cook I've ever had in my
life ! But I must honestly tell you that I think you
are taking this poor youth out of his proper place.
There was a very admirable precept—Hannah
More's, I believe—that was impressed upon me by
my grandmother, ' Never make a friend out of your
own class ' ! "

" I never heard anything so sickeningly early
Victorian in my life ! " said Katharine, yielding a
little ; it was impossible to her to fight with Jean.

" It's not fair to the friend either," went on Mrs.
Masterman, " in whatever reign he may happen to
flourish ; a Heart of Gold is all very well, but the
day comes when you feel ashamed of its owner,
socially, and that's fatal. It's impossible to argue
about these social differences, but there they are, and
everyone knows it. He may be defiant about it,
which is terrible ; or humble, which is worse. But
he never forgets it, and no more do you ! "

" My dear Jean," said Katharine, patiently, " I
respect these venerable truisms, but they're rather
beside the point. You make me an Anti-Socialist
lecture, merely because I resented a rude, stupid,
unkind——"

" Not as unkind as you are to poor Dumb
Crambo ! " interrupted Jean. " Have you considered that aspect of the affair ? "

"No, I have *not* considered it!" said Katharine starting up from her sofa, "I'm tired, and I won't be lectured any more! There's no Aspect, and there's no Affair, and if there were, I shouldn't consider them. And as for being unkind to Mr. Fitz-Symons, I can assure you he is the last person in need of your pity!"

"Here, sit down and be nice to the puppy, and I'll brush your hair for you," said Jean Masterman tranquilly. She said to herself that Katharine was one of the very few people who could look handsome when they were angry. She also wished that they had never come to Ireland.

CHAPTER XVII

IT was the fifth day of the frost. Each morning the sun had risen red through swathes of haze, glittered beautifully, and even warmly, in a blue sky, and hurried back to a more sympathetic side of the world. From its low zenith it looked daily into Dermot's box, and shone briefly upon him, as he stood, double-rugged, in the monumental silence and idleness that horses are capable of supporting without losing their reason. For him short rations had to take the place of daily exercise, as Tim, sitting on the kitchen table, and eating a meringue, observed to Parkington.

"Unless herself would be in it I wouldn't leave him outside the door. Where'd I be if he broke his knees on me? She'd have my life."

Dermot, therefore, occupied himself by gnawing the woodwork of his box by day, and by kicking his door, solemnly, in the depths of the night. He received, with a faint surprise, a daily visit from Mr.

Adare, who presented him on each occasion with two lumps of sugar, and made the regulation enquiries as to his health and appetite, events which, as they had not occurred before, he connected, not unnaturally, with the frost. They were occurring for the fifth time when Dermot pricked his ears at the sound of a footstep coming through the frozen yard, a footstep that was not Tim's, being both light and wavering, qualities quite incompatible with the soles of Tim's boots. Ulick Adare pushed the second lump of sugar into Dermot's mouth, and drew a quick breath. Katharine stood for an instant in the doorway, and Dermot raised his head and advanced to the door with a " Ho—ho—ho ! " of recognition.

" Why, he knows me, Tim ! " said Katharine, proudly, looking for the first time at the other occupant of the box. " Oh, it's *you !* " she said with a start, " I never expected to find you here ! "

Ulick found, to his great discomfort, that he was trembling. He took her hand and shook it as incapably as a schoolboy ; he could think of nothing better to say than a conventional inquiry as to how she felt.

" Oh, quite all right, thanks," said Katharine, in her pleasant voice, with a little more ease than she felt, " not worth asking after ! "

She was rather pale, but her colour rose as she spoke. She did not very clearly remember the afternoon of her accident—a fall on the head is wont to have an obliterating effect upon the memory—but she had not forgotten their passage of arms, and the fact that he had inexplicably lost his temper over a matter that was not only a trifle, but was no affair of his. Katharine had, upon occasion, comfortably quoted the line, " Hell holds no fury like a woman scorned," but she had yet to understand that earth holds no wrath more fervent, and more self-righteous, than that of a young gentleman who is accustomed to the position of first violin, and suddenly finds himself relegated to that of second fiddle.

As it turned out, his wrath had been justified, but none the less she meant to be magnanimous.

" I think I like my own horse better than the grey mare, after all ! " she said, with a laughing and apologetic eye, as Dermot nosed at her hand for what he knew she had brought. Dermot's stable manners were a credit to his late owner; he invited familiarities with a pleasing mildness, and neither nipped, nor snatched, nor grimaced. Katharine leaned her head against his warm, silky neck, and felt the thrill of proprietorship, and said silly, affectionate things to him.

Ulick Adare regarded her in silence. He thought there could be nothing more graceful than the droop of her head, more bewildering than the blend of russet and hazy gold in her hair. Her hand too; he had never seen her caress anything before, and it made his heart hammer and his breath come short. Until a few days ago it had been her company and not herself that he wanted; some answering quality in her mind and manner, more than any mystery in her grey eyes. Now he could only remember that this was she who had lain helpless in his arms, and had seemed ever since to rest there, whose sealed face of unconsciousness he had stared into, whose eyes had at last opened, and looked up at him without any surprise at finding his so near. She was with him again, and she seemed to have forgotten it all; had she forgotten that moment of precious nearness, or had she ever even known of it ?

Katharine noted his silence and glanced at him; he looked ill, she thought, not like himself.

" You know I have often told you that no one ever takes advice," she said, looking away from him; it was not easy to her to apologize. " People only learn by experience. That's what I have done."

The grey eyes steadied and looked straight at him.
" I'm afraid I was horribly rude to you——"

Adare came nearer to her and put his hand on the
horse's neck beside hers.

" If I had it to do again," he said in a voice that
wavered downwards as if it had been shot in the
wing, " I wouldn't let you go. You might be as
rude to me as you liked ; it would be better than
torture." The last word was almost inaudible.

Katharine took a step backwards, so sudden was
the shock, and so strangely mixed with it the instinct
to get away from him.

" That's putting it rather strongly," she said, red
to the roots of her hair, but still trying hard to be
commonplace.

" I thought you were killed," said Adare, in
a whisper, and stopped. " I didn't know," he
stammered on, " I didn't know, till then, that if
you were gone—I mean, it was then that I found out
what I'm trying to tell you—and I can't do it——"

He took her hand and pressed it against his
heart.

" Feel it ! " he said, " it's trying to speak ! "

It spoke indeed ; it was like a prisoner trying to
break his way out. Her hand was at his lips ; already
he knew it was a shrinking hand, but for that moment
it was his.

Nothing that Katharine had read and nothing that
she had thought was any help to her. This was love,
of which all the poets, including Ulick Adare himself,
had written, and it was not beautiful to her, nor
eloquent, nor compelling ; worst of all, it failed to
enlist her sympathy. It was merely bewildering,
and immensely distasteful. It was unthinkable that
this was the self-possessed, the entirely competent
Ulick Adare, bereft of voice, holding her every-day,
commonplace hand with a grip that hurt it. To
feel him kiss it, and kiss it many times, made her
cringe ; she drew it away.

" Don't take it from me! " said Adare. " Can you give me nothing ? "

" Not that," said Katharine, with difficulty.

She twisted her fingers in Dermot's mane, and leaned against his warm shoulder to steady herself.

She was taking it hard, as any one of her quality and perceptiveness would take it. Adare heard her shaken voice telling him to say no more, that he must forget that he had said anything, and she would forget it too. She said all that a generous nature, touched to softness, could say. She was dealing helplessly and conventionally with the greatest of miracles, and she shrank from its immensity. She was only a looker-on, moved, and yet unmoved, at the incredible sight of her friend, Ulick Adare, suffering because of her, and showing his suffering, as a man will to a woman.

CHAPTER XVIII

THE weather of Southern Munster does not count monotony among its failings. In five days it had arrived at the conclusion that the frost had created its sensation and was now a bore. It broke in the grand manner, and with the help of its boon companion, the Atlantic, piled up between sunset and dawn, a storm quite twenty-four hours in advance of the Admiralty warnings. After this there followed a week of wild and wicked weather, when the wind blew from the north-west, and the clouds, black as gunpowder, and charged, as with buck-shot, with hail and fierce rain, boiled up untiringly from some witches' cauldron, back of the hills.

It was, as it chanced, upon the day of the monthly pig-fair at Cloon, that the sun reappeared. It shone

with convalescent petulance upon the absorbed throng
of buyers and sellers, frieze-coated men and deep-
hooded women, a throng that probably pays less
attention to the vagaries of the heavens than is
yielded by any people who walk this lower earth.
Jerry Jacky Dunnigan, of Corrigilihy hill, had sold
his two fat pigs, and had bought a couple of *bonnives*
to reign in their stead, and had celebrated their
purchase in the classic manner. Not for an instant
is it insinuated that Jerry Jaky was drunk. He had,
according to the custom of the country, yielded up the
balance of the purchase-money to his wife, and she
had allowed him a shilling for *menus plaisirs*,
while she cheapened a pair of boots for her daughter,
and had what she called " a boxing-match " over " a
pair of pants for himself! "

It was during these operations that the elder
bonnive made his break for freedom. He and his
comrade lay in Jerry Jacky's cart, and regarded
the world through the bars of the crate that im-
prisoned them. The pig-fair was emptying itself
over the countryside, and an intermittent procession
of similar carts was leaving the town, loud with that
vast variety of grunt and shriek with which pigs
do not scruple to ventilate their grievances, however
transient and fanciful. It may have been some passing
cry to Liberty that fired the elder of the two bonnives,
or possibly it was the suggestions and allurements of
a green field that chanced to be opposite. Be that
as it may, he suddenly rose to his feet, and, with unearthly activity, sprang out over the top of the crate
and fell headlong into the road. A zig-zag scurry for
freedom and the green field followed ; Jerry Jacky
was summoned by a friend from his final public-house,
and in company with four volunteers, serious men like
himself, in dark blue coats and slouch hats, clambered
cumbrously into the field and entered upon the chase
with a slow and careful gravity, indicative of the
legitimate, pig-far condition of " having drink taken."

ı

There ensued in the green field a species of minuet, in which the bonnive, like a *première danseuse*, gave the time and set the measure. Again and again the five dark figures converged upon the bonnive, with the mesmeric stealth proper to such operations, and the bonnive, in perfect understanding of their intention, looked each pursuer in the face, set, as it were, to partners, and with a dazzling pirouette executed a fresh *pas de fascination*, and scuttled to new ground in another corner of the field. In the meantime the five wives, with other interested spectators, made an audience along the wall of the field, and delivered counsel, sarcasm, and epigram from beneath the deep and conventual hoods of their cloaks. Finally the bonnive darted through the legs of his opponents, left them swaying precariously in each other's arms, regained the high-road at a point clear of spectators, and made for the open country.

It was shortly after this that Mrs. Delanty, riding into Cloon on her bay mare, came into play. She had met the bonnive when it was beginning to weaken a little on the idea of liberty, and having perceived a pursuer afar off, had turned the fugitive aside into a timely farmyard. It was characteristic of Mrs. Delanty and her way of life that she should understand and act promptly in such an incident, and Jerry Jacky and his wife assured her that they had thanked God when they had seen that it was herself was out on the road before them. It was also in accordance with her habits that she should at once turn the matter to account by making searching enquiries as to the welfare of the fox that was wont to patrol the farm of Jerry Jacky on the high places of Corrigilihy.

" He's keeping the hill always," asseverated Jerry Jacky with vast solemnity and a steadying hand on the bay mare's neck ; " it's not on *my* land he'll be intherfared with ! "

" It wasn't but two nights past he was barking

around the house," interposed Mrs. Jerry Jacky, whose standard of description in social matters was higher than her lord's, especially than her lord's when in liquor. "I hadn't the hens hardly turned out in the morning before he had two o' them snapped ! "

The interposition availed nothing.

"Who's interfering with him ? " demanded Mrs. Delanty. "I can tell you there'll be no money for you for hens or anything else if he's interfered with ! "

Mrs. Jerry Jacky immediately adopted a new formation.

"Whoever is interhfaring with him it's not ourselves," she began, declaiming on a high reciting note. "Three ducks and a turkey he took from me last week, and a hen I took out of his mouth last Sunday, and she never laid an egg for me since, and if she didn't itself you couldn't blame her ! "

"Well, send in your claim, Mrs. Dunnigan, send in your claim," said Mrs. Delanty ; "but you couldn't ask me to pay for eggs that weren't laid ! Could she now, Jerry ? But I'll pay *you* a good ten shillings if we find the fox on your land ! '

"What signifies ten shillings ! " shouted Jerry Jacky, in a sudden burst of glory. "Yee can come on my land, and there'll be a welcome before yee, without any ten shillings ! And I'll have the gaps knocked before yee, and that's what more of them mightn't do for the Hunt ! "

It had already been obvious to Mrs. Delanty that Jerry Jacky was possessed of information that he desired to share with her ; it was also plain that, in accordance with the accepted method, he was determined to throw the lead into her hand.

"I heard something about Dunnigan Brieshka buying wire," she said tentatively.

"Did they tell ye it was prick-wire ? " said Jerry Jacky, with a blurred eye upon her face. "And how he have it rove through the bushes in the gaps ! "

" That's nice work ! " commented the widow.
" And did he tell you why he did that ? "

" Divil dang the word I spoke to him since Pether
an' Paul's day ! " said Jerry Jacky, first cousin and
next-door neighbour of Dunnigan Brieshka, once
more beginning to shout. " I'll tell ye no lie, Mrs.
Delanty, ma'am, he's a consecrated blagyard ! "

" I don't doubt it," said Mrs. Delanty, " but what
has he against the Hunt ? "

" What'd the likes of him care for the Hunt ! "
bawled Jerry Jacky. " It isn't twelve months since
he was in Ameriky washing bottles in a hotel ! "

Mrs. Jerry Jacky had by this time got herself and
the bonnive into the cart, and, seated in amity
between her purchases, was looking through the bars
of the crate with an expression in which wifely contempt for her husband and well-bred sympathy for
Mrs. Delanty were smoothly blended. The bay
mare, who had throughout felt offended by the
proximity of the bonnives, was beginning to fidget.

" There was a share of grazing land over-right the
station, that the Dunnigans had this long while back,"
began Mrs. Jerry Jacky with an apparent change of
the conversation. " Sure there wasn't one in the
country wasn't jumping mad for it, in regard for
it being so convenient to the thrain——"

" Quiet, mare ! " said Mrs. Delanty, as a bonnive
thrust through the bars a pink snout, flat and round
as a coin. " Brieshka got too cute in America, and
I suppose he thought he'd get it for nothing ! "

" Fitz-Symons was a match for him ! " guffawed
Jerry Jacky, moving somewhat deviously towards
his horse's head ; " an b'lieve you me there isn't a
dam one in this counthry, but he's a match for——"

" Yerrah, man, come home out o' this ! " said his
wife. " Ye have the lady bothered with your chat ! "

Mrs. Delanty rode on into the town, considering
the matter.

The aftermath of the pig-fair still wrought in the

streets ; the widow rode slowly on her business from
shop-door to shop-door, sometimes, according to the
genial methods of country shopping, pressing a
passer-by into her service, sometimes pushing the
bay mare upon the pavement and rapping on the
window with her cane, in order to attract the attention of the shop assistants. These, albeit pale and
harassed by combat with the country women, sprang
with undiminished civility to the summons. Mrs.
Delanty knew exactly what she wanted, knew in
what shop it could be procured, and knew also what
she was going to pay for it ; therefore her marketing
was accomplished with the least possible friction.
Her gladiatorial gift was held in reserve for great
occasions, such as a rise in bacon ; her bills were
small, and were paid regularly, a method which may
command the respect of the country shopkeeper,
but lacks the prestige of an outstanding account.

She was in the act of reproving the butcher for the
undue proportion of bone in his last consignment,
hastily, because during these complicated processes
she had come to the conclusion that she would try to
see Johnny Fitz-Symons before she went home, and
talk to him about this business at Corrigilihy, when
a couple of country women, broad and slow-moving
as barges, passed, on a full tide of conversation,
between her and the butcher.

" ' Faith ! ' says Tom Carthy, says he, ' 'twas little
but you were dead ' ! says he ! " narrated one of the
barges.

" Glory be to the most high God that He should
make such a thing and place it on the earth ! "
responded her consort.

" ' Didn't ye hear the horn, me good woman ? '
says the young fella' to me. And sure what horn
was in it only the little black ball they screeches
with : ' And if I head it itself, sir,' says I, ' how
would I know it was to me you were screeching ? '
says I, ' sure I thought it was jollying yourself you

were I ' Well, after all, he gave me half-a-crown, the poor fellow ! "

Mrs. Delanty leaned forward and caught the speaker's eye.

" Were you saying there was a motor-car in the town, ma'am ? " she asked politely.

" There is in throth, ma'am," responded the narrator, " and it's standing below at the hotel, and plaze God it'll not come our way ! "

" Oh, my mare's not afraid of it ! " said the widow, genially.

" Why then she's not like ourselves ! " said the country woman with a big laugh. " Faith ! I'd run through a kay-hole from it ! "

Mrs. Delanty turned her mare and rode quickly towards the hotel. This was Fanshawe ; he was, no doubt, on his way to see her, and there was nothing in the house for him to eat.

She was only just in time. He was already standing by the motor, putting on his gloves, when he caught sight of her. He came to meet her, and his colour rose by several degrees as he took her hand ; a tingle of self-consciousness, and of the pride of possession, brought an answering and eminently decorative tinge of carmine to the widow's cheek.

" You said you were to be out with the X.H. to-day ! " she began.

" Well—I'm not, you see ! " he said, gazing at her with a large and infantine admiration, " I thought I'd rather come and see you instead ! "

Infantine though Mr. Fanshawe might be, he had acquired sufficient astuteness not to mar the romance of this statement by mentioning that both his available horses were slightly " crocked," and in need of a day off.

" If you wanted to see me so much you might have let me know you were coming," returned the widow, arching her eyebrows and putting her neat little chin in the air, the while she thanked heaven that she had headed him off in the town. Whatever befell, he should not set his foot within the doors of her house this day. Were not Janetta and Kate this moment engaged in "turning-out" the drawing-room, happy in the prospect of a dinner of herbs and contentment therewith, after a week of stress in which they had had daily to prepare savoury meals for Mr. Fanshawe ?

"And now look at me on my way to the Fitz-Symons !" she went on, pettishly ; "I've *got* to go there on business, about the hunting, and what am I to do about you ? I can't leave a little boy like you playing about the town on a fair-day ! I hear you got into one scrape already, and it cost you half-a-crown to get out of it !"

"By Jove !" said Fanshawe, goggling at her, more like a devoted baby than ever, "you're a witch ! I say, look here, why shouldn't you lunch with me here at the hotel ?"

This was precisely the course that had already presented itself to Mrs. Delanty's mind, and after due hesitation she consented to change her plans, formed some thirty seconds before.

"Well, I dare say Mrs. Fitz-Symons doesn't exactly expect me——" she said ; which was indeed no more than the truth ; "if she hears where I was I'll tell her it's you she must scold."

She slid off her mare, evading his proffered arms, and followed him into the hotel through a group of pig-jobbers assembled at its door.

"I want lunch for two, please," said Fanshawe, addressing, as if she were the head-functionary at the Ritz, the pink-cheeked young lady in a white cap who met them in the hall. "What can we have ?"

The young lady looked at his fur-lined coat with apprehension, and faltered.

"The dinner's after going in, sir."

"Eh ?" said Fanshawe. "But I don't want dinner, I want——"

" Wouldn't whatever's ready do us ? " put in
Mrs. Delanty, who knew to a nicety the possibilities
of Burke's Railway Hotel ; " I'm sure whatever
Mrs. Burke's got will be very nice ! "

She advanced into the dining room, feeling pleasurably aware of her own smartness and even rapidity.
Her waist was very small, so also were her patent
leather boots ; she wore her little air of the condescending smart lady, to the entire admiration of
Mr. Fanshawe, if not of Mrs. Burke, who, from a
fastness in the inner hall, was viewing the proceedings
with understanding.

The dining-room was almost filled by a long table,
at one end of which three pig-jobbers were gobbling
roast mutton, and talking, with equal speed.

" Oh, I say ! Have you no place but this ? "
exclaimed Fanshawe.

" There's travellers in the room above, sir,"
murmured the waiting-maid.

" Ah, this will do well enough," said Mrs. Delanty,
still greatly condescending. " Sit down, now, Basil,
and don't be cross. You have all this end of the
table to yourself, and isn't that enough for you."

Fanshawe turned his enamoured eyes upon her.

" You're keeping your promise," he said in a low
voice. " That's awfully nice of you ! "

" Ah, it was only a half-promise, replied Mrs.
Delanty, pulling off her gloves. " I only said I
might do it sometimes, if you were good."

" Then I'm good now, am I ? " said Fanshawe,
seating himself very close to her at the end of the
table.

" Middling," said the widow, pushing her chair
an inch or so further away.

" I don't feel a bit good. I thought we could
have had a room to ourselves," complained Fanshawe.

" How bad you are ! " responded Mrs. Delanty,
who had found by experience that this particular
method of handling her young friend was exactly

suited to him. It compelled his admiration, and at
the same time bewildered him and kept him moving
a little beyond his pace. It was also the method in
which she had been brought up. What could a
large and simple young man from England, with a
slow-moving, logical mind, do against one of a family
of nineteen buccaneers, whose skill of the tongue had
been matured in that incomparable school of wits,
Irish third-rate society ?

The leg of mutton here appeared, snatched from
the table of " the Travellers " upstairs, an uninviting
hill of meat, with a gap in it like a railway cutting.

" Good heavens ! Can you eat this ? " said
Fanshawe, regarding with dismay this stalwart substitute for the little " luncheon " that in a vision
he had seen his chosen guest partaking of with
him.

" Of course I can ! " returned the chosen guest
with gallantry, while she in her turn thought with a
pang of Janetta's fresh eggs and well-brewed tea
and soda-bread. " Better than you can carve it, I
dare say ! Here, for goodness' sake, give me the
knife and fork ! I have a regard for Mrs. Burke
and her clean tablecloth."

Fanshawe watched her respectfully as she dealt
deftly with her task. He was like a big hound
puppy waiting for his dinner, and the widow, who
had walked many a one in her time, told him so.

" And if you stare at me like that I won't give
you a bit," she said.

" But I can't help staring at you," protested
Fanshawe. " I never met any one who could do so
many things as you can."

" Maybe, you never met any one before who had
to do them whether she could or no," replied Mrs.
Delanty, with an unwonted burst of candour.

There was something about Fanshawe that she
liked, quite apart from the glories of his money, his
strangerhood, his Englishness ; something good-

natured about him that even Janetta and Kate were
aware of.

The thought of the late Delanty crossed Fanshawe's
mind suddenly.   He wondered what sort of chap
he was, and if he had given his wife a bad time, and
whether she had been very sorry for him or not.

"Look here," he said translating his sympathy
into the form most obvious at the moment, "what
are we going to drink?   Let's have some champagne.
A fellow told me they had some stuff here that was
quite decent."

Mrs. Delanty hesitated.   Champagne was certainly
very smart, and it came her way about once in two
years.   On the other hand, there was no one to be
impressed by it except the pig-jobbers, and she felt
sure that it would go to her head in a manner most
unbecoming to her complexion.   It might also go
to Fanshawe's head, which would be very incon-
venient.

"I never heard such nonsense in my life!" she
said briskly.   "Champagne indeed!   At this hour
of the day!   You may have your whisky-and-soda
if you like, and I'll just have a nice little bottle of
ginger-beer."

Mrs. Delanty had been brought up in an atmosphere
of severe teetotalism, not because the Scanlan
family (of which, it may be recalled, she was the
youngest member) held a brief for temperance, but
because any drink more expensive than water was
a luxury as undreamed of among them as "late
dinner" or a second servant.

The meal progressed, and though destitute of the
graces proper to such an occasion, yet it had in it
something of the confidential quality that makes a
"little lunch."   Mr. Fanshawe found that he was
enjoying himself enormously.   He talked at great
length about his horses, about his grooms, and how
they fought with the "shover"; he told her of the
polo-ponies that he was going to buy, and of how he

wished that she would help him to do it, and the widow's soul instantly reviewed all the ponies of her acquaintance, and bought them at a price, and sold them at yet another price—a higher price—a much higher price.

Because all that Fanshawe said breathed unconsciously of money. The eldei brother who could " give him grass for his hunters in the park next summer " ; the mother with a house in London, which would be " handy for Hurlingham " ; the married sister whose husband had a pack of studbook harriers down in Kent.

" You know," he said, " this farming game is all rot really. I do it to please my mother. She thinks I ought to have something to do ; but I don't mean sticking to it. My notion is to take a pack of hounds somewhere——"

" Where ? " said the widow, quickly.

" Or—er—wherever they're jolly well fool enough to take me ! " said Mr. Fanshawe, with a pleasing simplicity.

" Oh, if it's fools you're looking for, you'll find them wherever you go," said Mrs. Delanty, from the lips out, as it were.

" He could take them without a subscription ; they'd be delighted to get him——" Her thoughts flew and stopped with a jar. What of John Michael ?

None the less her brown eyes beamed upon Fanshawe with a soft radiance.

" You'd look rather nice in a velvet cap, Basil," she said, " in spite of your long nose ! "

CHAPTER XIX

PORTER, Maggie! " shouted a pig-jobber, with his mouth full, " and hurry like a good girl! I see the people going down to the train ! "

He pointed out of the window with his knife, and Mrs. Delanty and Fanshawe, looking through the wire blind, saw an outside-car speeding by, with a man and his luggage upon it, and a bicycle tied across the back.

" Why, that's Mr. Adare ! " said the widow, with some excitement, " I didn't know he was going away."

" Oh, is he ? " said Fanshawe, who very much preferred the topic of the velvet cap. " All right ; I don't much care."

" Maybe you don't," said Mrs. Delanty, " but I wonder what Miss Rowan thinks about it ! Many's the walk I saw them taking together ! "

" Oh, I don't think Miss Rowan had much use for him," said Fanshawe, " he don't hunt, and she's mad keen."

" A pity she doesn't know more about it ! " said Mrs. Delanty, with a thin smile.

" She'll jolly soon learn," said Fanshawe, playing like the weaned child upon the cockatrice's den, " if she keeps on riding in John Michael's pocket in the way she does ! If you ask me, I think *he's* the fellow she has a fancy for."

" Well, you see, I'm not asking you," said the cockatrice, with a sudden heightening of colour and an infinitesimal laugh.

The weaned child was quite unaware of the imminence of her claws.

Ulick Adare meanwhile pursued his way to the station and took a ticket for Dublin. He had left

Lake View, not precipitately, nor with any kind of jerk ; one of the dark and age-long processes of the Irish Land Commission demanded his presence, and in obedience to its command he was betaking himself to his home in the County of Wicklow. He told his cousin that he was coming back again with an assurance that more than half imposed upon that experienced person. Katharine, as she stood at the door and saw him drive away, knew that he would certainly not return.

His demeanour throughout had been one of entirely diplomatic correctness ; his farewells were neither too long nor too short, too warm nor too cold. Katharine went back into the house and remembered without amusement, a story that he had told her about a painter friend of his, known as the Solicitor-General, who made a practice of proposing to young ladies, from artistic motives, because there was then to be seen an expression on a woman's face that nothing else would evoke.

" He will find the episode quite instructive," she said to herself in some bitterness of soul.

" Who sees when thou art seen least wise," says Milton, making, for him, a very unexpected confession when dealing with the eternal question of Man and Woman. Katharine had seen Adare when he had appeared to her least wise, moved by forces as elemental as those that, deep in a smooth sea, lift the ground-swell to its shattering on the rocks. It was mere blind force to her, but the remembrance of it disturbed and shook her. When she spoke to him there was a weight upon her eyes that made it impossible to meet his. Out of the depths of her own intense reserve she agonized vicariously for the giving away of Ulick Adare.

That Ulick Adare should apparently need no such attention was not the least disconcerting feature of the position. His social nerve she knew, but now, with mutual remembrance burning between them like a torch, she could not understand how he could be more at his ease than she. He took large walks in the wind and rain ; he withdrew himself for considerable spaces of time and dwelt apart in the important seclusion that is the privilege of men of letters ; he talked as much as usual, even more than usual, Katharine thought, with a metallic quality that was just perceptible to her. It was obvious that he was covering his tracks with all speed. She reflected upon another man who had asked her to marry him, and had less immediately accepted the position. He had married someone else the following year, so it all came to the same thing in the end, she said to herself, and quoted to herself the line :

"He will love thee half a year, as a man is able,"

and tried to remember who had written it, and thought she would ask Ulick Adare, and then reflected that that would hardly do.

The weather, which was still wallowing in the first excesses of the thaw, did nothing to assist the situation.

"The key-hole piped, the chimney-pot
A war-like trumpet blew,"

and the smoke burst in gusts into the rooms and filled the Pom with unappeasable alarms. The household was thus flung as it were into its own arms, and Mrs. Masterman, aware of tension in the social atmosphere, found herself in conversation, taking, like Falstaff, all the points into her target. That Katharine should be absent, tired, and heavy-eyed was very displeasing to her, but she ascribed it to the thrice-accursed affair of the grey mare and John Michael. She wrote letters to her friends of a length that at once assured the more experienced among them that she was very short of occupation ;

and to William, in far Rawal-Pindi, to whom she
confided that Lake View and everything connected
with it had been a vast mistake, and that Katharine
seemed bent on making a fool of herself, and, only
that it suited the children so wonderfully and was so
incredibly cheap, she would fly. To all of which
William, as is the way of the absent, responded with
an account of his last polo-match, and casually
added that he was glad to hear that Katharine had
taken to hunting, and that as for her buckeen, why
shouldn't she amuse herself if she liked. These
observations, however, arrived two months later,
when their value was not what it once might have
been.

"Rain or no rain," remarked Mrs. Masterman,
looking hard at Katharine on the second evening
after the latter's return to ordinary life, "you are
not going out hunting for another week if I can
prevent you."

"I shall go as soon as the weather gets better,"
said Miss Rowan, with almost excessive serenity.
She had become aware of a steady under-current of
opposition to the hunting, and, through the hunting,
to John Michael.

Ulick Adare made no attempt to support his
cousin ; he even mentioned that the glass was rising.
It was quite clear that she was to understand that her
going out or staying in was a matter of no moment
to him.

"It won't do me the least harm," continued
Katharine, with that flash in the brain that compels
people to say foolish things. "Naught's ne'er in
danger ! "

Jean Masterman looked from one to the other,
and, determined that there was more in it than met
the eye, and, quite unjustifiably, thirsted for the
blood of John Michael.

Three days after this Ulick Adare departed, and
the somewhat slothful calm that descends upon a

household of women in the absence of man fell upon
the Lake View establishment. Katharine began
again to exercise Dermot on the roads, and daily
came home with a headache, a circumstance which
she did not deem it necessary to mention. She was
in disgrace, subtle and unexpressed, and she knew
it, as it was intended by Mrs. Masterman that she
should know it.

CHAPTER XX

THE morning came at length when Katharine
sat at breakfast in her habit and felt again
that superiority to ordinary life, that magnificent
self-engrossment that is not often achieved by
women, but has been from all ages the privilege of
the Sportsman. Mingled with it was an uncertainty
as to how soon and how badly her head was going to
ache, and an accompanying certainty that if Jean
had even a suspicion of how slack she felt, she would
lock the hall door.

It was a grey and windy morning, with pale gleams
of sunlight, and the moist mildness of the westerly
wind in it ; the roads were buttered with a paste of
grey mud, and in the hollows of the fields splashes of
water were set like little mirrors for the sky. Dermot
had drawn his own conclusions from an early feed,
and from the extra pains bestowed upon his toilette,
and by sidling and pulling, rampantly, idiotically,
and exhaustingly, proclaimed his knowledge that he
was going to see the hounds again.

At Mrs. Delanty's gateway was Mrs. Delanty
herself on her bay mare, skilfully opening and as
skilfully closing the neat white gate that her own
hands had painted. She greeted Katharine with
her grander manner in the ascendant, the manner

which with her was generally indicative of a new hat, or a young horse successfully " passed on." Success was in the poise of her head, patronage in the arch of her eyebrows.

" You're not looking at all the thing," she remarked as they rode on together, " I think you'd have done better to stay at home." Her disapproving eye travelled downwards to Dermot. " That fellow looks as if he was short of work. I'm thinking you'll find him rather too much for you to-day."

" He's been exercised as much as possible," returned Katharine with humility, taking a shorter hold of Dermot, and descending two pegs in her own estimation, as her preceptress had intended that she should.

Mrs. Delanty had indeed travelled far from that primary position of Little-Dog-in-waiting to Katharine and Jean Masterman. She had become their patron, their interpreter to the country, and that the country should have lost no opportunity of extolling to her Katharine's prowess in the hunting field, her own especial domain, coupled with assurances that they had never thought the horse, *her* horse, had it in him to go like that, was naturally trying to a lady-patroness.

" I hear Johnny Fitz-Symons is greatly pleased with that grey mare that gave you the toss," she went on. " I declare I never heard of such a mad act as him to let a beginner like you up on her ! If he wanted to try her under a lady, that wasn't the way to go about it, and so all the country's been telling him ! "

It is often the intention to be rude, rather than the form taken by the rudeness, that produces the desired effect. In this case words and intention were fairly well matched, and Katharine retaliated after her kind by remaining silent and regarding Dermot's ears, with the annoying rise of colour that is the penalty of a fair complexion. In Mrs. Delanty's

K

class warfare of words is frequent and unimportant, but silence was a weapon with which she was unfamiliar, and it alarmed her. It also awoke an inner and deeper trepidation. " Could it be that she's gone about him ? " she thought, reading the red ensign after her own fashion.

" I have Mr. Fanshawe's horse in my stable still," she began, with a change of subject so swift as to indicate a sense of danger. " Indeed I might say that I had his owner there too ! I never know the moment I'll not hear his old coach-horn at the gate ! He says he's taking a veterinary course with me ; I make him work hard for his pass, I can tell you ! "

" I dare say he finds it very interesting," said Katharine, coldly accepting the proffered topic, not because she was at all placated, but because it saved trouble ; " especially as he doesn't seem to have very much to do."

" That's exactly what I'm telling him," said the widow, springing back, in the elation of the topic, to the position of confidential friend ; " that farming he's supposed to be learning is all humbug and nonsense. I never saw a gentleman yet that made money out of farming ! No ! But what'd suit him, and what he'd like, would be to have a pack of hounds."

" But does he know anything about it ? " said Katharine, who had not been specially impressed by Mr. Fanshawe's abilities in any walk of life, " and could he afford it ? "

" He'd soon learn if he had the right people to teach him," said the widow, with an air of very special knowledge, " and as for affording it——" She relapsed uncontrollably into her native grade of the Anglo-Irish dialect (and grades there are many). " Sure he's rolling ! Two thousand a year, my dear ! And more when the mother dies ! If he couldn't keep hounds on that down here, it'd be a queer thing ! "

" Down here ! " repeated Katharine, suddenly
interested, " what country could he hunt here ? "
Mrs. Delanty hesitated elaborately.

" I wouldn't be surprised—— " she began, approaching, with hushed footsteps, the subject that was to
her the most momentous that life had to offer, " if
there was to be changes here ! I hear a good deal
—you see—I don't know how it is, but really, people
seem to tell me things they mightn't mention to
another ! " She paused, and was so engrossed in
her subject as to squander upon Katharine one of
the glances that she was in the habit of bestowing
upon other and more appreciative objects. " I'm
afraid—— " she laughed a little, " the farmers aren't
as fond of poor Gus Fitz-Symons as he thinks they
are ! "

" Do you mean there are political difficulties ? "
said Katharine, still with slight severity.

" Oh, gracious, no ! " said Mrs. Delanty, " this is
a different thing altogether. He's mixed up in a
row about grazing with some of them, and he's lent
money to more, and Mr. Gus has ways of his own
about getting it back ! He has the Dunnigans up
against him now, and that's half the country, you
might say ! It's a very different story with the
farmers now since they've bought the land ; it's hat
in hand me friend Gus should be to them."

" I thought the covert we were to draw to-day was
on Dunnigan's land ? " began Katharine, " a man
with a curious name, Brieshka, I think Tim called
him. Does Mr. Fitz-Symons know about it ? "

Mrs. Delanty became rather red.

" Indeed *I* don't know what he knows or what he
doesn't know," she said with her lightning utter-
ance, and with unexpected heat ; " if he and Brieshka
fall out it makes very little difference to *me* ! *I've*
had enough of patching up Gus Fitz-Symons' quarrels
for him and getting no thanks for it ! "

Katharine remained silent. The distaste of the

Clan Dunnigan for Mr. Fitz-Symons was not difficult to understand, but she was not going to say so to Mrs. Delanty. She also thought that that lady's attitude towards her friend was quite what might have been expected.

"Of course Gus is an old friend of mine," went on the widow, perhaps divining disapproval, "but I must say I never liked him very much."

Katharine laughed, in spite of her extreme desire not to do so.

"Oh, thank you!" she said, "I've so often felt that, but I've never been able to express it!"

The widow stared in mystification, and, as she disliked being mystified, she said with some asperity that it was getting late and they had better trot on.

Up at the Pike Cross where the hounds were waiting there was a fierce wind blowing. The horses, standing with their backs to it, had their tails parted down the middle by the blast; the hounds, established under the lee of the fence, sat in a sapient row, and licked the mud off each other's faces; the riders sat with hunched shoulders, and, each in the order of his arrival, grumbled to his neighbour that it was outrageous to wait for people, and hounds ought to stick to the published hour. Mr. Fitz-Symons on his brown horse loomed large against the cloudy sky, and returned the salutations of his Field with majestic and bilious gloom; it was the general opinion that old Gus had got out of bed on the wrong side. John Michael and Tom Coyne had been aware of this misadventure from the moment of its occurrence, and were now awaiting the events of the day with a resignation born of the knowledge that whatever fate might bring forth, they would be in the wrong.

The Master advanced to meet Katharine, and made her his felicitations on her reappearance; he informed her with *empressement* that he had waited for her, always a two-edged kind of compliment, and one entirely typical of him. He further told her, with a sour glance of his muddy brown eye at John Michael, that he had told his brother what he thought of his conduct; he shouted it against the wind, in order that his views should be thoroughly ventilated, and the widow giggled audibly in the background.

There are moments when the flame of wrath is quite disproportioned to the match that has lighted it. Katharine's head went up and her back stiffened; without a word she rode up to John Michael, and greeted him with such a warmth and such a kindling light in her grey eyes as scared him to the marrow of his bones. She inquired ardently after the health of the grey mare; she declared that she was longing to ride her again, and, like the Master, she took care to speak in so loud a voice that those around should be in no doubt as to her sentiments. In short, she overdid it thoroughly, and gloried in it.

John Michael fidgeted in his saddle and gathered up his reins.

" I have Tom Coyne out on the grey mare," he said hurriedly, with his eye fixed on his elder brother, " she's doing grand. I think he's moving on now— War' horse there, Bluemaid! C'up, hounds! "

They went on up the old coach road, broad and wind-swept, and turned at an acute angle into a farm lane. There was a long pond that lay in shelter at the corner, and Katharine, from her place in the string of riders, saw the red coats and the patches of white that told of the moving pack, reflected brokenly in it. The dead fronds of the Osmunda fern were reflected too, in restless confusion of yellow and brown; some of the hounds splashed through the reeds at the margin, and sent a coot skimming away down a flashing, splashing path, and scared a tall heron into wide-winged creaking flight. Tom Coyne, on the grey mare (transformed out of recognition by desperate doings with the mane comb and the clipping-machine) cracked his whip and shouted at the straying hounds; John Michael blew a long note on his horn to warn

late comers that they were moving on, turning half
round in his saddle to count his field.

> " The huntsman loosens on the moon,
>   A gay and wandering cry,"

thought Katharine. " How can anyone say that
sport has no place in art ! "

" Any one " was Ulick Adare, who might or might
not be pleased at being thus remembered. Her eyes
were dim, the pulses of her head throbbed. She was
over-strung, and the beauty of the world and the
excitement of living in it were almost more than she
could bear.

The hunt paced along the lane, two and two, between the high banks ; advancing like a motley troop
of cavalry, towards the oak-wood on Corrigilihy Hill,
where lay their adversary, alone and self-sufficing,
prepared at any instant to pit his solitary resource
and daring against theirs. They halted in a narrow
valley between low hills, covered with yellow and
grey oak scrub ; they were in shelter at last, and the
men lit cigarettes, and the horses plucked at the grass
on the bank above them, as if they had not had anything to eat for a week. There were not more than
a couple of dozen out, and Mr. Fanshawe's and Mrs.
Delanty's were the only voices that had not been
subdued by the aspect of the Master. Mr. Fitz-
Symons had notably the gift of inflicting his ill-humour
on all in his vicinity ; sheer magnitude of sulk, and
the indifference of Juggernaut as to consequences,
creating an effect that was artistically complete.

A hound said something in the thick covert on one
side of them, a note of conjecture and uncertainty,
but the horses pricked their ears and looked up,
with disreputable wisps of grass and bits of twig
hanging from their mouths. There was silence for a
moment, except for a steady rustling and bustling
in the stiff undergrowth. Then, a hundred yards

away, the same hound spoke again, and others joined him.

" That's like it ! " said some one near Katharine in a low voice.

There was a strip of sward below the lane, between it and the trees, and it was precisely there that to Miss Rowan was vouchsafed her first view of that good-looking gentleman of many aliases, Dan Russel the Fox. He came out of the yellow and grey scrub as imperceptibly as a drifting leaf, sighted his enemies of the second degree, and withdrew as delicately and discreetly as he had come, a soldier of fortune, perfectly acquainted with his danger, and meeting it without a touch of panic. The covert again swallowed the chief player in the tense and intricate game of wood-craft, and the Master started at a clattering gallop up the lane, presumably to look for his huntsman.

" It's no good staying here," said the man who had spoken before, " now they've got a move on that lad he'll go on."

" Listen ! " said some one else. " They're at him again ahead there ! Isn't that the horn ? "

They pressed on, a disorderly mob, in the direction taken by the Master, Mrs. Delanty and Fanshawe in front, the widow with her inimitable air of knowing exactly what was happening and where she was going, Katharine close behind them, with every faculty concentrated upon finding the hounds and the hunts-man, and cleaving to them and to them only.

Hapless Huntsmen ! Few but they can know what it is to be the star to every wandering barque, the pilot to every emulous beginner ; stars entirely preoccupied with illuminating their own concerns, pilots only anxious to steer a course as remote as possible from their adherents !

The lane, such as it was, presently faded away in an open space, where the grass ran in and out among outcrops of grey rock that looked like the backs of

half-buried elephants ; gathered on one of these was
a family of goats, whose yellow eyes, filled with grave
indignation, spoke of recent shock. Further on, a
couple of cows, gaunt and long-horned, of the old
Irish breed of brindled black and red and white, were
staring over a barricade of branches and brushwood.

"That's the way John Michael's gone," said Mr.
Clery, pulling up and regarding the barrier with
respect.

Hoof-marks led up to it and reappeared on its
further side ; other hoof-marks led to it and turned
away to the right.

"I've seen a good horse staked in a better place,
and I happen to know the people here have no fancy
for having their fences destroyed," said Mrs. Delanty,
also turning away to the right. "Keep your eyes
open for barbed wire, all of you ! There's no use
going there, there's a good way further down on
Jerry Jacky's land ! "

"Begad, you're right ! " said Mr. Clery, who was
not in the last ashamed of having common-sense.
"They're not running, anyway, and that's an unnatural ugly sort of a place ! "

Mr. Clery's opinion was one that might be creditably
accepted by any one, but Jimmy Doyle did not follow
his lead, and Katharine, making one of the myriad
small decisions that seem trivial, but are, in hunting,
momentous, elected to follow Jimmy Doyle.

"I think there isn't much time to lose," he said,
sliding off the black mare, and dragging a sort of
Christmas tree from the barricade. "But there's
no sense in being a fool ! Be Jingo ! but Mrs. Delanty's no fool either ! Look at that !

Two strands of barbed wire strung across the gap
were revealed as he pulled the branches away.

"That's a nice little cat's cradle for you ! I wonder has Brieshka many more of the same sort before
us ! " He was already tearing out of the barricade
the post to which the wire was attached. " There,

that'll do now," he said flinging it on one side. " It's
well for Johnny Lottery's a big-jumped mare ! We'll
be minding ourselves now till we're out o' this, I
can tell you ! "

Brieshka's Christmas tree was replaced, and, in
the silence and solitude that presently followed,
was minutely examined by the cattle, with the in-
exhaustible inquisitiveness of their race. The barbed
wire now decorated the boughs of a tree ; the brindled
cows saw it there, but none the less, though good
fencers in an ordinary way, they respected the barricade.

" I say, Lily ! " said Fanshawe, as he followed
the widow with calf-like fidelity through a slit in a
furzy bank and along the headland of a tiny patch
of turnips—Mrs. Delanty was always careful about
crops— " I hope we're all right."

" I told you before I wouldn't have you calling
me that in public, or anywhere else ! " replied Mrs.
Delanty, casting a look at him over her shoulder that
made him ride up beside her and say ditheringly—

" You darling ! "

" I suppose you think that's an improvement !
I won't let you come hunting with me again if you
can't behave yourself ! " retorted the lady of his
affections, while selecting with an unerring eye her
gap in the coming fence. " And look at you now !
Destroying Brieshka's turnips, as if he wasn't cross
enough already ! "

Following upon her words came the sound of voices
in altercation, loud, and infuriated, one of the ugliest
sounds in the realm of nature.

" Oh, my goodness ! That's Gus ! There's a
row ! " cried Mrs. Delanty in a breath, her dark eyes
lighting in the irrepressible Irish love of a shindy ;
she dealt the bay mare an awakening whack, and
hurried like a street boy to the core of the situation.

In the next field a group of battered trees, their
topmost branches blotted with the nests of a colony

of rooks, strained stiffly in the wind ; beside them was a two-storey cottage, new and hideous, a bare grey box, with an eaveless slate roof, and four windows, hard and staring as unsympathetic eyes ; the dreary, utilitarian substitute for the long, low cabin, with the uncertain angles, and the kindly, motherly thatch, and the little, friendly winking squares of glass peering out from under it. In the gateway of the yard was a man with a pasty and freckled face, and dull red hair that twisted in corkscrew curls about his forehead. Added to these attractions were eyes of the colour of ripe white currants, lit at this moment by the flare of fury. Facing him was the Master on his horse ; they were baying in each other's faces like dogs. The red-haired man was shouting in a voice that had the crack of rage in it, and the American twang running through it, like the barbed wire through the branches. He shouted over and over again that no Fitz-Symons should ever cross his land. The Morse alphabet of dots and dashes alone could adequately render Mr. Fitz-Symon's response. Two colts, who like the Master, were anxious to get through the gate, were flourishing round his horse, neighing, squealing, and kicking. The big west wind rushed through all, deafening, and buffeting, intensifying, as is its wont, the output of temper.

" Come back ! " said the widow to Fanshawe. " He'll get no good of those people—don't *you* mix yourself up in it ! They can have us all up for trespass if they like—look at the mother coming out now ! "

Mrs. Dunnigan, senior, was indeed taking the field. She advanced from the door of the house with her arms extended, and her brown shawl hanging from them like outspread wings ; a cap-frill, and an encircling red "shawleen," framed her fervent countenance. She thrust herself in front of her son, and in a scream that topped the wind she launched the catalogue of her own wrongs. Hens were in it, trespass was in it, and above all, the Gogginses were in it.

("They're the earth-stoppers," explained the widow, in the background.)

The Gogginses were, it appeared, the biggest brats that ever Ireland reared, the dirtiest thieves that ever God framed. Her native sense of rhythm lent balance and swing to the saga. She said that the marks of their legs were down on their little potato-garden; that whether she'd go aisht the road, or wesht the road, theirselves would be watching her, as black as any dog, and that it wasn't but last Sunday she melted them under her teeth with cursing. She paused, by a simple modulation, from the Goggins family to their employer. The scream took a higher note to match the greatness of the theme. She extended her arms and swept them downwards to the ground, in illustration of the fact that she cursed Mr. Fitz-Symons from head to foot. She told him that the like of him never swept the country before, and that there wouldn't be a good word, or a good wish, or a good prayer after him—here the colts, making a determined rush to get past the Master, jostled against him and his horse, and he turned and brought his crop heavily down on the woolly back of the nearest colt. The colt flinched under the blow, darted forward through the gateway, followed by his comrade, knocked Mrs. Dunnigan into her son's arms, and both into the gatepost, and fled away round the house.

In a second Brieshka had the Master's brown horse by the head, and was kicking him in the chest, and the Master's whip was again in the air. That it failed to descend upon Brieshka was due to the exertions of the brown horse in the cause of peace. He shook him off with a rear and a plunge, pivoted on his massive hind legs, and blundered in among the horses of the lookers-on. It was during the plunge that Mr. Fitz-Symons began to fall off; the process continued during the pivoting. The members of the Hunt watched, as men watch a land-slide, powerless and appalled, while the Master lay upon the neck of the brown horse, clasped it in vain, and, with gathering impetus, progressed down his shoulder to the mud. Immediately old Clery and the other men closed round Mr. Fitz-Symons ; the brown horse, still with outrage in his eye, recovered his self-control, and the Master, with his cap over one eye and his thong wound round his neck, clambered back into his saddle.

" You're witnesses, every one of you ! " he bellowed, with what breath was left in him. " He assaulted me ! He'll be in jail for this ! I'll go home and take out a summons this minute ! I'll take the hounds home—— " He tore the horn from his saddle and tried to blow it, but had only wind enough to produce a cracked and disastrous bleat. He turned his horse and galloped out of the field by the way he had come, while the valedictions of the Dunnigans rained upon his retreat with the blended lavishness and precision of a machine-gun.

CHAPTER XXI

IN the meantime, the first cause of these disturbances, that leader of society, and moving spirit in its feuds and friendships, Dan Russel the Fox, had slipped from one patch of covert to another, running up wind before the patient advance of John Michael and his hounds, until he had crossed the last of the little ridges and valleys into which the tail of Corrigilihy is shredded ; once he met with a little boy, minding sheep, who threw a stone at him, and vaunted himself of the feat to John Michael ;

once he met a lady of his own race, who put him a
part of his way before she ran back into the wood
(and three and a half couple of hounds turned back
with her). And once he paused near the back door
of a cabin, and—John Michael being half-a-mile away,
interviewing the little boy—considered the question of
meeting his teeth round the neck of a white duck,
and retiring with her to a certain drain in the vicinity.
This, however, was interfered with by the owner of
the duck, who flung a sod of turf at him. (And she,
too, was subsequently a help to John Michael.) At
about this point a note of the horn travelled to him,
thanks to the fact that he had manœuvred himself
into the position of being down wind with relation
to his pursuers, and being a philosopher, he accepted
the position and laid himself out to go.

The narrative presented to John Michael by the
woman who owned the duck was as brilliant and as
irrelevantly decorated as the page of a missal. He
heard it with the patience that experience had taught
him, and having sifted from it the fact that she had
last seen the villyan going east past the school, he
gave her one of his few shillings, and she screamed
" God speed ye ! " as he lifted the feathering hounds,
and galloped with them to the school house.

Yet at the schoolhouse they hung, puzzled, as if
the wild wind had whirled the scent away with it.
The children, out for their play hour, decked the
walls of the school-yard as vividly as flowers, red and
black and golden heads, scarlet cheeks and bright
eyes and bare pink legs and arms ; they squealed
and gabbled and hissed in sibilant chattering, as only
Irish National school-children can. But they had
nothing to tell John Michael about the fox.

It was here that Jimmy Doyle and Katharine,
travelling express via the little boy and the owner of
the duck, got on to the main line, and at the same
time Tom Coyne was developed out of space in the
act of towing the grey mare over a fence whose

complex problems might have given pause to a rabbit.

"Master Johnny!" he called, "there's three and a half couple gone back into the wood with another fox, and I'm told there's been the divil's work with Brieshka, and the Master sent a message to me to tell you you're to bring the hounds home the quickest way you can!"

John Michael faced his mare about quickly. "What's that you say?"

Tom Coyne repeated his message with all the glory of his kind in "bloody news." Katharine with wisps of fair hair blowing into her eyes, and her crop shoved under her right knee as she endeavoured to deal with her coiffure, turned upon Jimmy Doyle a countenance that had the blaze of the wind and the gallop in it.

"If I were he I shouldn't go!"

Jimmy Doyle grinned.

"Maybe he won't either!"

John Michael, at home, was all that a subservient younger brother could be, but John Michael with a fox in front of him was as capable as Nelson of putting the telescope to his blind eye.

"I can't stop them now," he said shortly, standing in his stirrups to look over the bank by the road side. "They have it right this time! Come up! mare!"

The hounds were indeed away again, and Tom Coyne, with a comfortable smile said to himself, "Well, I done my part anyway!" as he pushed the grey mare after the chestnut one, and shook her up to gallop her best after the pack, now sliding as smoothly over the grass as a cloud shadow.

Once more for Katharine was the dream and the delirium; the brown heather and the green fields, the lounging, sprawling banks, no two of them alike, the truculent, challenging walls, all were merged into a rushing stream; every jump was a flash of

triumph, every fair space of grass a sailing glory.
It seemed the easiest thing in the world, and the
finest, to ride in John Michael's wake, to catch his
eye as he looked back to see if she were safely over,
to feel that he and she and the hounds had but one
heart among them.

The slopes of Corrigilihy were far behind them
now, and the schoolhouse was no more than a white
dot in the past, when the hounds checked for the
first time at a road, a long empty stretch of dun-
coloured road, that wandered between bogs and
low hills, and served no apparent purpose of agri-
culture or civilization. There ensued a delay, un-
accountable, mysterious. The eager hounds spread
themselves with every appearance of conviction
over a chocolate-coloured expanse of peat-mould,
with deep pools in it, and spikes of bog-wood standing
up out of the black, wind-ridged water, and long
turf-cuttings grooved with the marks of the " slân."
Up from it came the aromatic, complex bog smell ;
sea-gulls, driven inland by the weather, swirled and
screamed above the hounds.

" We're done with the good country now," said
John Michael to Katharine, with an unprecedented
burst of confidence. " They ran him nicely when
they got on terms with him, back at the school,
didn't they ? "

Katharine, overwhelmed by the surprise of a
personal appeal, replied with a *feu-de-joie* of the
most impassioned superlatives at her command.

" There isn't a little pack in Ireland that'll hunt
better than what they do when they get their chance,"
went on John Michael, with the light in his eyes
that only hunting brought to them. " They took
him out of the wood in a hurry ! I'm glad you
didn't miss it."

John Michael was decidedly uplifted by his gallop.
He met Katharine's reverent eyes unflinchingly,
and was moved to yet further commendation.

" I never saw a lady to go as well, and you on a green horse too ! "

" I should have been nowhere if Mr. Doyle hadn't shown me the way out of the wood," said Katharine ; approval from John Michael was a gift so large that she could not accept it all.

" The rest o' them didn't catch us yet ; " said Tom Coyne, casting a jubilant eye back over the empty country through which they had come ; " and it'd be hard for them ! As for this mare, she's running away with me ! "

This may or may not have been intended to mask the fact that the grey mare was puffing considerably, and was black with sweat where she was not white with foam.

" Them hounds are doing no good below there, sir ; will I whip them out of it ? "

" You will not," said John Michael.

There were three of Mr. Fitz-Symons' hounds whose word was law, and these were Reckless, not as young as she had been, Admiral, tall and grey-muzzled, and the incomparable Rachel, whose least hint, it is little to say, was more revered of John Michael than all the wisdom of the ancients. Rachel it was who made a great hunt out of what had been a smart gallop, but had not Reckless and Admiral put their noses down to that one faint whiff that she had detected some thirty yards up the road, and snuffed long and thoughtfully over it, with ears hanging over their eyes, Rachel might not have considered it worth while to pursue the matter further. Slowly, almost pensively, she strayed onwards. A bare out-crop of rock kept her for quite a minute, and Admiral and Reckless joined her again.

" I *may* be mistaken," she said dubiously, with rigid stern, snuffing like a vacuum cleaner.

" No, you're not ! " said Reckless, giving a small, thin squeal that the wind blew away, unheard save by Admiral.

He came up, stood motionless for a moment on his four bed-post legs, and put his grey nose down; then raised his shabby, handsome, old head, and uttered a single commanding bass note, which, being interpreted, meant:

" Pipe away, all hands ! "

" There you are now," said Jimmy Doyle, in a voice sad with the whole of pleasure, " that's the hunt."

" It was the road he ran after all," assented John Michael.

In what fashion, however, he ran the road was one of the mysteries of scent. Judging by the procedure of the hounds one would have said that they were following the leaps of a kangaroo, so completely did the scent fail here, so entirely sufficing was it there. For about half a mile the road yielded an intermittent inspiration, while the wind blew sweet and strong across the wide bogs, and the hurrying sky broke up into companies of clouds, and a sun like a silver ball slid among them.

" This check's just what the horses wanted," Jimmy Doyle said to Katharine, as he and she, their brotherly love still continuing, moved side by side at John Michael's heels, and the black mare, in sourness restored by leisure, made faces at Dermot like an angry cat.

" I suppose the rest of them's belting round the wood with that three and a half couple," proceeded Jimmy, sociably ; " that's unless they went home with old Gus ; Tom Coyne's after telling me that of all the rows Gus ever had, and he's had plenty, this flogs the lot ! " He squeezed the black mare up beside Dermot, and looked sideways at Katharine from under the flat brim of his pot hat. " I wouldn't be surprised to hear he chucked, and I don't blame him in a way. He knows well that what all the country's saying is that *he* "—he jerked his head at John Michael—" he's the Master, and Gus is the pay-master ! "

L

" It works very well," said Katharine, the wind whistling in her teeth.

" Well, y' know," returned Mr. Doyle, " it's poor fun paying the piper when you've a wooden leg."

" Every bit of him is made of wood ! " said Katharine, scornfully.

" It is. And rotten wood too," agreed Jimmy Doyle.

This seemed to dispose of Mr. Fitz-Symons, but the interest of the topic was for Katharine and her boon companion practically illimitable. Those of Katharine's friends who were wont to accuse her of excessive and wilful fastidiousness, would have been entertained at beholding her, wind-ruffled, flushed, and voluble, riding along a bog road with two buckeens of low degree, deeply immersed in the affairs of a cultureless, not to say barbarous, community, quite oblivious of her own axiom that hunting need not be confused with hunting people.

John Michael held up his hand ; the hounds, after a final hesitation on the road, scrambled over a stone gap, bringing it rattling after them, and began to bustle ahead at a pace that looked like business at last. The ground rose towards a long ridge of hill, with sometimes a squashy bank, sometimes a drain muffled in briars, sometimes a little slatey wall, wandering in the sedge, and looking as if it were built of cards ; more often, as the valley was left behind, cattle-passes revealed themselves and were accepted by the party with gratitude. There were indeed now but three concerned. Tom Coyne and the grey mare had been turned back by the grey mare's owner, and had been last seen on a road, trailing disconsolately homewards, like a dog that has been driven back from church. (And why all dogs should so greatly desire to go to church is a matter for a committee of bishops and veterinary surgeons to decide upon.)

Fifty yards ahead of the others Lottery pursued

her way at a steady trot over the rough ground ; if Katharine deviated from her leader's track she found herself in difficulties ; it was as though there were but one way, and John Michael had trodden it from childhood. She began to apprehend, dimly and for the first time, the varied gifts that are needed in getting over country like this without a pause. It was a long and inexorable trot ; as time went on, and the seemingly tireless hounds carried their wavering banner of music across the wide hill-country, she found herself thinking less of whether Dermot would last, and more as to whether she herself could stand it much longer. She who had always regarded a weak back as an almost moral defect, and was quite aware of the straightness and suppleness of her own, now found that she was drooping in her saddle, weighed down by something that was not merely fatigue, that was worse than fatigue, a creeping sense of weakness, a feeling that if she let go for a moment she would lose her courage.

"An hour and fifty-seven minutes ! " exulted Jimmy Doyle, as they stood in the shelter of a ruined cottage and watched the hounds, again at fault   " I declare I could be sorry for the rest of them that we left after us ! I think the fox has us beat for all that," he went on, as the hounds wandered onwards without conviction, and with not more than a hint of scent vouchsafed at intervals. " It was that check on the road saved him."

They moved ahead and upwards into thin, low heather ; advancing at a walk, they topped the ridge of the hill, and the wind rushed upon them, with the damp and smell of the sea in it, and huge grey clouds drove across the lesser grey of the sky, like a herd of charging elephants intent on some titanic chase of their own. Below were long dreary slopes of heather, stretching away illimitably ; over the edge of the world, Katharine thought. This was the shortest day of the year, and it seemed to her the longest, though even already the threat of darkness was in it. There was nothing worthy the name of sunset, but a yellowish glow on the western clouds told that the sun was nearing the unseen Atlantic.

"That's File-na-Showk!" shouted Jimmy Doyle against the wind, pointing with his crop to a peaked hill that rose darkly in the west. "You can see that from the hill back of Lake View."

Katharine looked at File-na-Showk, brown and forbidding in its naked nearness, and recalled the blue and delicate shape that she had seen one sunny morning, across the curves of lesser hills, and remembered how a man cutting furze had told Ulick Adare what its name was. It all came back to her very clearly. Ulick Adare had said its salient spike was like the Dent du Chat, and they had then looked down at the little lake below them, and conceded that for blueness it must yield to Lac Bourget. They had talked of La Chambotte, perched high on its precipice above the lake, of its tea and hot scones, its vision of celestial Alps, seen through the haze ; of the tiny strip of braid below, where crept, between mountain and water, a tiny caterpillar that was an express that had thundered its way through the Mont Cenis. "*Our* expresses are donkey-carts!" she had said, "and I much prefer them!" She had also told Ulick Adare that he would never know what Irish scenery could be until he came out hunting with her and Mrs. Delanty.

"You're fifteen miles from home this minute!"

Katharine came back with a start from High Savoy, and was aware that Mr. Doyle was regarding her with a compassionate grin.

"Johnny never knows when he's had enough. I think it's time for me to tell him he's lost a couple of shoes, and indeed I may say you're no better yourself!"

He left her and rode to the lonely figure that was

moving steadily onwards ; the two red coats borrowed strength of colour from the dull glow of yellow in the west, and with self-assertion and with tyranny subdued the brown and grey wilderness into a background for themselves. The hounds were scattered widely in front of them, searching, and still searching, for that which was lost to them.

John Michael put his horn to his lips and blew a long and cheerless note.

" Home ! " he blew. " Home ! "

And Dan Russel the Fox, lying very tired and dirty, under the lee side of a rock half-way up Filena-Showk, heard the long note, and said to himself that he was done. He arose stiffly, and listened with pricked ears, and stared down across the valley with yellow intense eyes, that were by this time rather back in his head.

It was some little time before he allowed himself to believe that the odd trick was his.

CHAPTER XXII

A MORE thoroughly thwarted individual than Mr. Fitz-Symons, junior, could scarcely have been found in the Province of Munster.   He had not accounted for his fox, he was short three and a half couple of hounds, perhaps left behind in Corrigilihy, perhaps at this moment running the line of their comrades, being chivvied by cur-dogs, or enticed into captivity by country boys with a view to reward. He was fifteen or more miles from kennels, and there was the delay of getting the horses shod. He said to himself that if it wasn't that Lottery's hoofs weren't the best, he'd chance it, but there'd be row enough with Gus as it was, without bringing the mare in lame.

He was, at this point in his meditations, engaged in pushing his muddy, discomfited hounds into a shed at the back of the forge ; he felt certain that there would be hoof-parings in it, which they would fight over, eat, and make themselves sick with. Among the three horses there were five shoes gone, and, no matter what the smith said, he knew it would be a good hour before he had the five " slippers " on them. John Michael, though an easy-going person, kicked the sagging door of the shed savagely in order to induce it to shut, and thought to himself that, as the delay was on him, he might as well have a cup of tea as well as another.

There was a thatched cottage near the forge, the private residence of the blacksmith, and John Michael directed his steps towards it. It was noticeable that he walked as easily and ordinarily in his hunting-boots and breeches as in any other costume, He neither straddled, nor hobbled, nor conformed with any other convention of sporting gait ; he merely walked. He had tramped in them for miles in deep furze and tangled woods, and the process had conferred ease alike upon them and their wearer. It was the hopeless thing about John Michael that he had no professional airs, no airs, indeed, of any kind, which is a serious disadvantage to penniless youth, however good-looking.

It was twilight, and there was a light in the window of the smith's cottage. John Michael opened the door and walked in out of the cold fierce evening into a glow of firelight. It was a large and roomy cottage, with an earthen floor, and a big, blackened chimney-place with a projecting hood like a long upper-lip ; the fire was on the hearth, a turf fire that had been reinforced with scraps of coal and a crow's nest of broken twigs, through which the blades of flame grew up like grass. Above, in the blue, clambering smoke, a kettle hung and sang in burly joviality. Katharine was sitting on a kitchen chair by the hearth, her profile very pale against the dark chimney corner. She looked at John Michael as he came in with the look that people give to those they have been expecting, whether consciously or unconsciously, and in response to it John Michael came gingerly in and sat down on a chair with his back to the wall, like a servant at a registry-office.

" Wouldn't the gentleman come down to the fire ? " said the smith's mother, looking at John Michael with a jolly eye. She was kneeling at the hearth with a large brown tea-pot in her hand, and above her stood Jimmy Doyle, warming one muddy foot after the other. " Sure ye're dead, the whole kit o' ye ! 'Tis yee that got hardship ! "

Katharine moved her chair a little to one side to make more room.

" Not much hardship, I think ! " she said, looking at him with a smile that said more than she knew. Over-fatigue is like slight drunkenness: it weakens the powers of concealing emotion, sometimes, even, it awakens emotion.

John Michael came forward with his cap in his hand, looking more than ever like a Spanish gipsy.

" It's the poor hounds got hardship ! " he said, sitting down on the settle at the opposite side of the fire, " to lose their fox after all ! "

He looked at Katharine with more of comradeship than he had yet ventured, and thought to himself that it had been too big a day for her entirely, her first time out after that concussion. He remembered that he had had practically to lift her off her horse at the forge.

" I'm afraid it was you got the worst hardship," he added.

" It was worth it ! " said Katharine, with another of those unguarded, charming, tired smiles.

" I wonder will you be thinking that this time to-morrow ! " said John Michael, regarding her almost as kindly as if she were a hound.

" I don't care what I feel like to-morrow," said
Katharine, " I've had my hunt ! "

" And you rode it well too ! " said John Michael,
warmly.

Jimmy Doyle, looking down upon them, said to
himself, " Hullo ! hullo ! hullo ! Johnny, my lad,
maybe you're not such a fool as we think ! "

Here the smith's mother informed them that the
tay was wet. The chairs were dragged across the
hills and dales of the earthen floor to the table under
the window ; the wind rumbled in the chimney, and
wrangled shrilly outside with the fuchsia hedge with
a sound as if it were whistling through its teeth.
The lamp flared in the draught from a cracked pane.
Turf-smoke and salt struggled for supremacy in the
butter, the bread tasted of the box in which it resided
with the bacon ; yet as Katharine sat at the end of
the table and wielded the big tea-pot with a stiff
and tired arm she was aware of the strangest content,
of something that was lulling, and even enchanting.
She was in an oasis, with the rest of life away at the
far edge of the wilderness. She was in the bright
ring of the magic-lantern, and everything else was
in darkness.

The three hunters, following immemorial prece-
dent, talked of the run, and of it only, mile by mile,
almost jump by jump. To Katharine it was all
horses, to John Michael it was all hounds ; Jimmy
Doyle maintained an illuminating course between
the two points. The seriousness of the two young
men, their decorum, their deference to her, gave
Katharine a peculiar and most subtle thrill. She
met, with a delight in its simplicity, John Michael's
clear and earnest gaze as he explained where, at a
critical point, Frantic had picked up the line, and
how Vanity had once gone near putting them astray,
only for his knowing that she might tell a lie, once
in a while, she might have lost them the hunt ; the
gravity of such a disaster was reflected in his face.

The attractiveness of simplicity is reserved for those who are not simple. Katharine saw him as if he were a picture ; his looks spoke to her of romance, his sincerity moved her like music, she felt that security and repose came to her from him. Strangely, through all, was blended the protective instinct. No matter how she hid it from herself, the consciousness of his class was always there ; it was as if he were a child, with some slight lameness or disfigurement, that she would shelter with a fierce tenderness. She wished that Jean Masterman were there, to see him as she saw him, and to have to confess that he was a gentleman in the oldest sense of the word.

A loud and startling rapping on the window interrupted this idyllic meal. In the small square of the window the face of Fanshawe was suddenly presented to them.

" Run them all to ground ! " he shouted through the wind to an unseen companion, " open the door ! "

Jimmy Doyle's chair fell with a clatter as he sprang to obey the summons ; the door opened, the shoulder of the wind driving it in, and Mrs. Delanty and Fanshawe came in on top of the gust. The idyll departed up the chimney (in the teeth of the smoke, which was coming down it), and the smith's mother said audibly—

" The Lord have mercy upon us ! I couldn't get another egg for them if I was to crack me neck for it ! "

There was that about Mrs. Delanty that spoke of tidings, a manner of importance, even of severity.

" We've found you at last ! " she began, with her eyes on John Michael, " you seem to be enjoying yourselves ! I suppose you don't know that the Master went home at one o'clock ? "

" Did anything happen to him ? " said John Michael.

" Plenty ! " said Mrs. Delanty, accepting as a tribute and without a remark the chair offered to her by the smith's mother (who afterwards in this

connection said to her son that That One had no
more manners than belonged to her).

"He's had the biggest row with Dunnigan Brieshka
that ever he's had with anyone," resumed the widow.
"He sent the Field home and told them he'd never
take the hounds out again."

Silence followed this announcement, and every
one looked at John Michael, who maintained a
steadfast countenance.

"He asked me and Mr. Fanshawe to find you and
tell you you were to come home at once."

"Well, I'm coming," said John Michael, shortly.
"Had he any hounds with him ?"

Mrs. Delanty's face changed.

"He had two and a half couple with him," she
said slowly.

"There's a couple away, so," said John Michael.
He had no desire to discuss at this juncture the more
momentous tidings; "they'll come home all right."

Mrs. Delanty hesitated; she understood very well
how much she was going to hurt him. Quite suddenly her eyes filled with tears.

"It was Sindbad and Fantasy," she said with a
choke. "They picked up something on Brieshka's land."

"Poison ?" said John Michael, quickly.

She nodded her head.

"Was nothing done for them ?"

"We did all we could," said Mrs. Delanty, putting
her handkerchief to her eyes; "butter, and all sorts
—it was strychnine—they were too far gone."

"That settles it," said John Michael, picking up
his cap and walking to the door. "I'd best see if the
horses are ready."

Mrs. Delanty followed him to the door.

"Reveller picked up a bit too, but I think he got
the emetic in time. Mrs. Clery took him straight to
Ashgrove in her pony-trap."

"Did any more get it ?" said John Michael, standing still, with a face of stone.

"No, no, no!" she said eagerly. "That was all
—just those three."

"Look here, Fitz-Symons," said Fanshawe, "is
there nothing I can do for you? Help you to get
the hounds home, or anything?"

"Doyle will do that," said John Michael, dully.
"I'm obliged to you all the same."

"Johnny," said Mrs. Delanty in a low voice,
putting her hand on his sleeve, "every one knows
there's no spite against *you*!" Her dark eyes were
brimming as she looked up at him.

"What good is that when they poison my hounds?"
he said, opening the door cautiously, so as to mini-
mize the inrush of the wind.

She was very close to him as he released the inside
latch and took hold of the outside one.

"I'm sure you did your best, anyway," he said.

"I'd do more than that for you, Johnny," she
murmured, with an impulse as strong as the wind
that sprang in at her.

She had a moment of meeting his eyes, and the
trouble in them, before the door closed.

"May the divil flog Dunnigan Brieshka's soul to
hell!" said the smith's mother, who was a woman
of wide sympathies.

CHAPTER XXIII

THE night was very dark. The wind blew in
power, and the heavy-laden sky fled before
it. It was behind the tired hounds and horses
and riders as they moved along the dim roads;
it swept them on; it roared in their ears like a river
in flood. Now and again a young moon, furtive
and curved like an Eastern knife, thrust her blade
through the confusion of clouds, mastered them for
a moment, and was overwhelmed. The miles of road
yielded themselves up slowly and grudgingly, and

with every mile the fatigue, that had been something mitigated by rest and food, settled again like
lead upon Katharine. She and her two companions
seemed to be the only human beings who had not
been blown into shelter. Here and there a yellow
star shone across the dark country, out of unknown
heights or hollows, with inevitable mystery and
suggestion. People were there, fortunate, sheltered
people, above all, stationary people ; people whom
fate did not compel to advance endlessly through
darkness, as she was doing, cramped in one unalter-
able position, with a back that responded painfully to
every shuffling stride of the tired horse.

An age or two passed—in silence, because the wind
made conversation with Jimmy Doyle too difficult.
The half-seen figure in front came to a stop.

" Jimmy ! D'ye know which is the road ? "

Katharine perceived that they had come to cross-
roads of indeterminate character.

" I forget is it here we turn off ? "

John Michael's southern, high tenor voice cleft
the wind as only such voices can.

" I d'no ! " yelled Jimmy, " I'll ask at the house."

One of the yellow and mysterious stars had re-
solved itself into the light of a cottage away to the
left.

" Better be sure than sorry," he said to Katharine.
You have enough before you still, without our losing
the way for you."

Dermot strayed on, and Katharine found herself
in the middle of the hounds, who, with their huntsman, had pressed close under a high bank for shelter.

" It's a long road," said John Michael. " There's
a short cut we might take, but I'm not too sure of it
in the dark."

" How much farther is it ? " she asked.

" It mightn't be more than another six or seven
miles," he said compassionately. " I'm afraid
you're dead."

"I *am* very tired," said Katharine, yielding to a sudden and irrepressible craving for his sympathy.

"That's too bad! It must be that you're feeling that fall a bit still."

He spoke with concern, as well as with the respectfulness that so continually touched her, and hurt her too.

"I used to think nothing could tire me," she said; "but now, somehow——" There was a catch in her voice, and she broke off. "I'm talking of myself," she said, "and it's really you who are to be pitied, with all this trouble about the hounds——"

"It cannot be helped," said John Michael, using the invariable formula of the peasant when sympathy for the irrevocable is offered. "I'm sorry you didn't stay at the smith's house with Mrs. Delanty," he went on in his serious voice. "We could have sent a car for you."

"I much preferred riding," said Katharine, recognizing the guileless good intention of this somewhat ungallant speech, and replying to it with an equal sincerity.

Here Jimmy Doyle's voice came to them out of the darkness.

"It's the left-hand road, and you'll go through the end of Drumcoora Wood."

They continued their journey, and Katharine rode beside John Michael.

The wind resumed its bleak tyranny, and flying wisps of rain scourged them as with the lash of a knout. Tired as they were, the horses quickened their pace of their own accord; the road slanted downwards into a glen, and presently the shelter of Drumcoora Wood enclosed them as suddenly as if they had entered a room. The rush of the wind was in the branches high above their heads, but on the road it was still as if they were under the sea. It was profoundly dark, and Katharine, riding on John Michael's left, felt Dermot draw close

to the chestnut mare as if in need of companionship.
That which was hot at Katharine's heart found its
opportunity.

" I wish I could tell you how much I feel for you,"
she broke out. " I mean about the poisoning of the
hounds. There is something so brutal about it—I
know how you must feel it ! "

There was a pause.

" I'm not saying they were the best I had," said
John Michael, with his invincible simplicity, " but
it cuts me to think they'd die that way, and me not
there to do what I could for them."

" Oh ! I understand that so well ! " said Katharine
ardently.

John Michael received this assurance in silence.

" The worst thing about it," he resumed in a
lifeless voice, " is thinking any one in this country,
that I thought was so friendly, would go to lay
poison before hounds. I wouldn't mind them
having a bit of a row with Gus. That's nothing
new."

" What will happen ? Must the hounds be given
up ? Why should you have to suffer for other
people ? " said Katharine, charging into the heart
of the matter.

" This looks like a notice to quit, anyway," said
John Michael.

" It wasn't meant for you," she said impulsively.
" Any one can see—I can see myself—how much the
people like you ! "

" It's Gus that owns the hounds," said John Michael
after an embarrassed silence.

" It would be all right if you were the Master !
You know that ! " said Katharine, with a burning
determination to pierce his armour of respect and
humility. For the first time in her acquaintance
she heard him laugh.

" And Gus to pay for them, I suppose ! He'd
like that ! "

" It's very much what he's doing now ! " said
Katharine, hotly. " Why shouldn't he help you ?
Think of all you've done for him ! "

" He'd not do it," said John Michael, with complete finality. " And I wouldn't ask it from him
either."

Her intense fatigue played its treacherous part in
breaking down her sense of proportion ; the loneliness and darkness pressed on her ; she wanted his
kindness, his strength ; she was quivering with his
wrongs, yet if she had laid her head on his shoulder,
it would have been in defeat, not in championing.

" Let *me* help you," she said in a voice into which
tenderness escaped in spite of her.

He made no answer. She could not tell if he
heard her or not. The road had turned sharply
at the end of the wood, and the wind rushed at them,
broadside on, across the shuddering breast of the
country. It shouted in their ears, it drove between
them in intolerable egotism, and in it came the rain.

CHAPTER XXIV

MRS. FITZ-SYMONS went heavily, yet ener-
getically, upstairs, for probably the fiftieth
time that afternoon. She bore in one hand a cup
of hot milk and in the other a bottle of brandy ; her
countenance was perturbed, her cap rode aslant on
her heated brow. She crossed the landing, and
went down into a narrow passage, filling it comfortably from wall to wall. Stopping at a door she
pushed it with her knee.

" Now, Mary," she said, " come on and we'll give
him this. It's a full half-hour since he had the last.
What way is he ? "

" You'd say he was nicely, ma'am," replied Mary.
" There wasn't a stir out of him since I came up."

This was not altogether what Mrs. Fitz-Symons
desired to hear. She deposited her burden upon a
table, took up the small lamp that indifferently
lighted the room, and held it low over an old sofa
in a corner by a stove. The young hound, Reveller,
lay there, extended on his side, one would have said
lifeless, so prone and motionless he was, so deadly
white the skin round his eyes and about his muzzle.
He had had less of the strychnine than his comrades,
the crucial attacks of convulsion and rigidity had
passed, and were now succeeded by the scarcely less
crucial condition of collapse. As she stooped over
him, he lifted his eyelids towards her, and made a
little movement of a hind leg, all the welcome he
could put forth from under the weight of weakness.

" Poor Reveller ! " she said, laying her fat, motherly
hand lightly on his side ; " poor puppy ! I wish I
had the blackguard here that put you this way !
Come on, Mary, he's in want of the brandy."

The sick hound yielded to their ministrations,
because he was too weak to resist.

" Run away now, girl, and see is the fire lighting
well in Master Johnny's room. My gracious goodness ! Dy'e hear the rain ! What in the wide
world is keeping him, I don't know ! Look at the
hour it is, going on for nine o'clock ! "

Mrs. Fitz-Symons gave to the little stove the
niggling poke that is all that is possible in dealing
with its mean tribe, and seated herself in the room's
solitary chair, by the room's solitary table.

It was a small room, on the borderland between
a servant's bedroom of the pre-historic type and a
lumber-room ; it had a skylight instead of a window,
cobwebs instead of curtains. It was the lair in which
John Michael preserved such personal matters as the
remnant of his medical books, his horse and hound
medicines, ancient, and highly odorous hound-couples,

and sundry articles of horse clothing which he held
in reserve, concealed from even Tom Coyne. It was
over the kitchen, and in close touch with the back-
stairs, and in consequence of these privileges was
used by its owner as a nursing-home and private ward
for the kennels. Mrs. Fitz-Symons took her knitting
out of a black velvet bag that hung at her side, and
resolutely composed herself to patience. Her broad
brow had lines of distress in it, and there was more
than a tinge of red round the open blue eyes that
kept so gallantly the flag of youth flying in them.

She had been through deep waters since her step-
son came home that afternoon, and she knew that
even deeper were in front of her; Gus was not
going to stop the hunting and stop the hounds without making some one sorry for it, and the first and
the last person whom he would make sorry for it
would be Johnny. Mrs. Fitz-Symons here closed
her mouth very tightly, then, knitting hard, opened
it again and whispered to herself various repartees
that she would launch on behalf of her Johnny, when
the hour of the deeper waters was upon her and him.

The sick puppy panted and stirred a little; she
went to him and put a thermometer within the fold
of his fore-arm, stroking his feeble opposition into
quietness while she did so, and thought that you'd
hardly know which it was you were nursing, a dog or
a Christian, only that the dog was much the best
patient. She studied the thermometer at the lamp,
with her spectacles on, and found that the gleaming
thread of silver touched a point higher than at the
last record.

"Well, that's something good to tell Johnny,
anyway," she said.

As she was putting it away there arose to her from
among the vague noises of the kitchen below the
voice of Mary.

"The horses are after coming up to the front door,
Ma'am!" it proclaimed.

M

" Up to the front door ! " repeated Mrs. Fitz-Symons, starting up.

She had had one shock that day, and her knees were shaking under her as she hurried out of the room and down the passage. " Is it an accident ? " she thought, and then—" Johnny ! "

The hall lamp was flaring in the draught from the open door ; she looked down into the hall, and saw a tall woman standing there in a riding-habit, her hat shining with rain.

" Who's that ? " cried Mrs. Fitz-Symons. " Has anything happened to Johnny ? "

" *He's* all right," replied the surly voice of her step-son. " This is Miss Rowan. Come down."

" Thank God ! " breathed Mrs. Fitz-Symons, as she descended.

Katherine was standing with her hand on the hall table, as if to steady herself.

" My goodness, Miss Rowan ! are you all alone ? " exclaimed Mrs. Fitz-Symons. " Where's Johnny ? "

" He's gone on to the kennels," said Katharine ; " he insisted on my coming in, I was so tired and wet. He said I might ask you if you would kindly let me go home in your covered car. I'm afraid I can't ride any further——"

Mrs. Fitz-Symons gave a single swift look at Katharine's white face.

" I'll kindly do no such thing ! " she replied, putting her hand on Katharine's sodden coat sleeve ; " why, my patience alive, child ! you're drowned ! "

The master of the house shut the hall door with a bang, an act which might, by a stretch of imagination, possibly be construed as signifying his acceptance of Miss Rowan as a guest.

" It's a pity he didn't insist on your coming in a little sooner ! " he said ; the bitter rage that had been fermenting in him since the morning loaded his glance at Katharine, and every line of his face showed black under the unsparing top-light of the lamp.

Some sub-section of her brain perceived that his evening attire took the form of a tweed suit, too shabby to wear in the daytime ; she was also aware that he smelt of whisky and tobacco. It was a smell entirely appropriate to him ; intolerable, after the pure anger of the wind and rain out of which she had come.

" I'm very glad he didn't," she said, defiantly, " we've had a wonderful run ! "

" It's the last run, wonderful or no, any one'll have with *my* hounds ! " retorted the Master, loudly ; " when my hounds are poisoned, and my huntsman refuses to obey my orders, it's about time for me to pitch the whole show to the devil—and I wish I'd done it long ago ! "

Mrs. Fitz-Symons pushed Katharine towards the stairs :

" Come up, my dear ! Come up this minute and get those wet things off you ! " she exclaimed, volubly interposing, " sure your teeth are chattering in your head this minute ! A good glass of hot punch is what you should have ! "

Mr. Fitz-Symons swung into the dining-room and banged the door.

" You may bang your doors, me laddie-o ! " said his step-mother to herself, dauntlessly. To Katharine for the honour of the house, she said with a large wink :

" He's vexed now, and when men are that way it's no use talking to them—and indeed, to tell the truth, he got bad treatment to-day ! Don't bother your head now about anything ; Jimmy Doyle will leave a message at Lake View for you on his way home."

For half an hour the household of Ashgrove wrought in a fever of ministration to Miss Rowan. The inevitable bucketful of live coals was conveyed from the kitchen and emptied into the grate of " the spare room," a genial method, whose instant efficacy atoned for the attendant smoke clouds that tracked its passage through the house. Genial also was the ready flame of the bogwood that was lavishly added. Mrs. Fitz-Symons and Mary ran like excursion trains, heavily laden ones, between the kitchen and the spare room, conveying tea, soup, punch, blankets, at five-minute intervals. At each entry a battle was fought with the lock of the door.

" There's no keeping it shut, bother it ! " said Mrs. Fitz-Symons, banging it ineffectually for the twentieth time. " I'm tired asking the carpenter to mend it ! Indeed the last message I got was from his wife. ' If he was in love with you,' she says, ' he couldn't mend it for you, he's that busy ! ' "

At the end of the half-hour, Katharine was reclining in an armchair, in front of the fire, attired in a flowing *robe-de-chambre* of Tyrian purple, provided by her hostess, while Mary timorously, and with heavy breathings, dried and brushed her wet yellow hair.

Katharine had written to Mrs. Masterman the most conciliatory explanation that her frozen brain and fingers could accomplish, but she was aware that Jean was not going to be pleased. Again she wished that Jean could be with her, to see what these people, whom she so sedulously undervalued and misunderstood, were really like, and how superior was their hospitality to the tepid toleration of the professional hostess. She was intensely and overwhelmingly tired ; she could not think, except in snatches, but the creature that is behind thought hung her brain with pictures. She lay there obsessed by images of John Michael. She saw him wet and tired feeding his hounds, while his stepbrother lay in wait for him in that den into which he had slammed himself. She saw his grave face, his shy, kindly eyes, his light figure in the shabby

red coat ; she felt his strong hands, and their gentle-
ness, as he lifted her off her horse.

Mary crept out of the room, and hastened down
stairs to inform the kitchen that the young lady was
kilt tired altogether, and was gone asleep, and God
knew she had as much hair on her head as'd fill a
bolster.

Katharine slept, profoundly, motionlessly, with
her hair in a cloud about her pale face, that always,
in sleep, was both sweet and severe.

" Indeed," as Mrs. Fitz-Symons afterwards said,
" she was a picture, there in the chair. As handsome a girl as ever was in this country, and the
stamp of high breeding on her, and I'd hold to that
if it was my dying breath ! "

It was Mrs. Fitz-Symons herself who disturbed
Katharine's repose.

" I'm come to put you into your bed, my dear,"
she said, " I don't hold with your sleeping in the
chair this way. It's eleven o'clock. I saw the light
in the crack of the door."

Katharine came up out of oblivion with a wrench,
and her surroundings jarred into their places with
a jerk, like badly handled stage scenery. It had not
been good sleep, it was unpleasant sleep, with lead
in it, and there was a fog in her head, but she noticed
almost immediately a difference in the aspect of
her hostess.

" Has your son come in ? " she said, putting her
hand to her head as if to clear it.

" Is it Johnny ? " said Mrs. Fitz-Symons, with a
pant in her voice as of recent stress, " he's in this
hour and a half. Didn't you hear them talking ? "

She looked hard at Katharine.

" I heard nothing," said Katharine, casting her
mind back into that dark pit of sleep.

" It was himself and the brother," went on Mrs.
Fitz-Symons, the candlestick shaking in her hand,
" the first time ever I knew Johnny to answer him

back!" She sat down abruptly. "Oh, Miss Rowan, my dear, the hunting's done, and my boy is going from me!"

Katharine sat up in her chair. "Going!" she repeated, with a tone in her voice that penetrated Mrs. Fitz-Symons' own distress.

Mrs. Fitz-Symons wiped her eyes openly and unreservedly; she was candid in all her emotions and in the manifestation of them.

"Why wouldn't he go?" she said, "when his own brother told him he wouldn't keep him here eating his head off at his expense. There was a nice thing for one brother to say to another! And Johnny that worked for him day and night like a negro slave. He'll know the difference of it when he's gone from him."

"How could he say such a thing to him?" said Katharine, flinging away discretion. "It was cowardly—horrible."

Mrs. Fitz-Symons was again aware of an intensity of sympathy for which she had not been prepared.

"And to say it to Johnny! The gentlest creature that ever came into a house. Too gentle he was, and that's what I often told him. I had my answer for Gus. I told him up to his teeth, ' your poor father left me this house,' says I, ' for as long as I live, and Johnny shall stay in it while he pleases.' "

"Well done!" said Katharine, hotly.

"But what good is it for me," went on Mrs. Fitz-Symons, clenching her handkerchief into a ball, "Johnny says he'll go to America!"

The name that has cleft the heart of many mothers felled her courage, and her voice collapsed for a moment.

"He says there's a pack of hounds out there that's wanting a huntsman—a man that wrote about hounds was asking did he know of any one would go—he has it all planned."

Katharine lay back in her chair. It seemed as if the name of America had cleft her heart too.

" If this house is yours," she said at last, speaking slowly and steadily, while Mrs. Fitz-Symons again dried her eyes, " why shouldn't he stay here and keep the hounds ? He might be helped to buy them, and he could be given larger subscriptions."

" And who's going to help him ? " inquired Mrs. Fitz-Symons, with a streak as of dawn developing in the back of her shrewd mind.

" Every one would, I should think ! " said Katharine, still feeling her way, but with a quickened breath. " Any one who has been out hunting here might be grateful for the opportunity of helping him, after all that he has done——"

" They know well what he has done, and no thanks to them ! " replied the mother of John Michael, " but they'll not put their hands in their pockets for him for all that, and if they did they wouldn't find anything in them ! "

Katharine was silent, because she was trying to put forth in a phrase the hot and heroic schemes that were tumbling over one another in her mind. It seemed to her that she was like a huntsman trying to select one hound from among a baying kennelful of eager comrades. She had seen John Michael do it. She was full of the great stimulants of wind, and effort, and wide places ; the voices of the hounds still cried in her ears. Through it all she saw the face of Mrs. Fitz-Symons, moist and expectant.

" I could help," she said.

Mrs. Fitz-Symons, with the utmost difficulty, restrained herself from flinging her arms round Katharine's neck, and hailing her as her daughter-in-law. She was accustomed to the simple, financial point of view in matters of the heart, yet, as she looked at Katharine, something deep within her breathed a caution. With the unerring perception that belongs to her country she was intensely aware of that old-fashioned, intangible, invincible barrier of class; she recognized and reverenced it, in the turn of Katharine's head, in the turn of her thought, in every attitude of mind and body ; she even discerned in her that intellectual quality that had before now daunted the average youth.

"I know you would, my dear," she said, with a tremble in her voice, "and if there was any sort of a plan could be made, or any help we could ask from you, indeed we wouldn't scruple to ask it. Johnny said to me to-night he never saw a lady to take such an interest in the hunting as you did, nor one that'd ride out the end of a hunt like yourself."

Katharine's pale cheeks burned. "I only followed him," she said in a low voice.

"There's a great many wouldn't do that!" said Mrs. Fitz-Symons, proudly, "and I can tell you one thing, I never heard Johnny to praise any lady before. And what's more, he wouldn't say it of you if he didn't think it, not if you were the Queen!" She paused, and flung bogwood on the fire as though heaping an altar to her son.

"He was very kind to me," murmured Katharine, confusedly.

"Then I can tell you he was anxious enough about you," went on Mrs. Fitz-Symons, "as quiet as he is, there's very little that he doesn't see! He told me you have too much courage, and that you did more than you were able for."

The flame of the bogwood flared soft and tall, and Katharine put her hand over her eyes as if it hurt them. She had done her best, and he had understood it, and in the middle of his own trouble he was thinking of her ; it crept warmly to her heart.

"You're tired now," said her hostess, instinctively leaving off in the right place, "and you should go to your bed. It's time for me to go and look after my poor puppy ; I'll not let Johnny sit up with him to-night, no matter what he says! I declare the

storm's gone down.   Have a good sleep now!"
She closed the door as well as its incapable lock
would permit, and as she did so she said to herself.
" Please God, America mightn't get him after all !"

CHAPTER XXV

REVELLER fought for his life that night, or,
to speak more truly, the battle was fought
on his behalf.   For him the task of drawing each
faint and fluttering breath was enough, the swallow-
ing of the weary succession of potions almost more
than he could endure.

" Little and often ! " said Mrs. Fitz-Symons to
herself, as she once again lit the spirit lamp and
warmed up a brew of concentrated nourishment that
should reinforce the hard-pressed fighting line.   She
had nursed many dogs, young and old, since John
Michael, at the age of five, had brought in a little
piteous cur with a broken leg ; she had seen many
a hound-puppy, buoyant, radiant, a miracle of vitality
and joviality, in a few days and nights collapse
and vanish in that stupefying waste that Nature
would seem to sanction.   Mrs. Fitz-Symons could,
as she said, put up with Nature, but this was not
the hand of Nature, it was the hand of man, striking
in cowardly and stupid malignity at the innocent.

She shook her head over Reveller, and thought
he would hardly do ; none the less, she was not the
woman to give in till she was beaten, and Reveller,
who was the son of Rachel, was very dear to John
Michael, which was enough for John Michael's
mother.

" If he lives over the turn of the night it will be
a wonder," she said, looking at her watch with eyes

dim with sleep. "Three o'clock! I don't care what Johnny says, I'll not call him."

She lifted Reveller's heavy, unresisting head, and putting a towel under his chin skilfully administered the meat juice and the brandy that he hated, yet swallowed, with the touching submission that is in itself a sign of ill omen.

"He'll do now till the half-hour," she said, talking aloud for the company of her own voice; "I'll run down and make a cup of tea before I go asleep standing."

A kettle was singing on the corner of the kitchen range; the rats were chirping like chickens in the blackness of the scullery, the cockroaches glittered as they fled before the light of her candle, but beyond turning up the skirt of her dress in a complete and effectual manner, Mrs. Fitz-Symons treated these nocturnal incidents with an accustomed calm. She made the tea, and sat down by the table to drink it, and knew the human relief of being removed from the inhuman presence of unrelenting illness, a commanding presence, even in the case of an animal. Sleep was fighting in her for the mastery, as if she had been drugged, but the tea drove it back; with a cleared brain she plunged again into those beatific visions of Johnny's future, that during her vigil, had beguiled her drowsiness.

She was, as she often said, "a great one for planning;" she had never, she told herself, known him to take as much notice of any girl before. As for giving tea to a lady, and riding home with her every step of fifteen miles, never, no never, would she have believed he would do such a thing, he, that had never so much as looked crooked at any one. "A kind of a nun of a fellow," Captain Bolger had called him once, and she had been ready to tear his eyes out at the insult. She wouldn't grudge Johnny to think more of his horses and his hounds than of girls and their nonsense, but a bit of a flirtation never did

any one any harm, and it kept great life in the place.
But, thanks be to God, she thought, with exquisite
satisfaction, this was more than a flirtation, this
was a love affair. With one stride her thoughts
travelled to the very house that Johnny should
take, the outhouses that could be turned into kennels,
the sheltered field that would make a flower garden
——The daughter-in-law, who was to accomplish this
transformation, played a somewhat nebulous part
in the vision, but always as a person of great distinc-
tion, commanding, throughout, the homage and the
jealousy of the neighbourhood. It did not seem
incongruous to her that, even in her inmost thoughts,
she could only think of her daughter-in-law as " Miss
Rowan."

She had sat there for nearly half an hour when a
sound in the room overhead made her start to her
feet with her hand on her heart. It was a low,
hollow howl from Reveller, long-drawn and wavering,
fraught with the uttermost of despair. It was not
the first time that she had heard such a cry from a
sick dog ; she had heard it once, at night, from the
stable where lay a hound-mother with her puppies,
and the morning had found the mother stiff and
cold among her blind and searching children. She
had heard it uttered by a young hound with distemper,
who had been brought in to spend the night by the
kitchen fire, and he too was dead when the morning
came. And once a little terrier, in the throes of
pneumonia, had in the dark of the small hours put
up a similar cry for help from its basket in her bedroom, and she had been in time to drive away the
vulture of death that it had seen hovering.

Remembering these things, Mrs. Fitz-Symons ran.
She lumbered up the steep back stairs, and hurried,
panting and heavy-footed, down the passage to the
sick-room. With all her speed, another had been
speedier. John Michael, in shirt and trousers, and
barefooted, was kneeling by the sofa,

"The brandy, Mother! Quick! He's alive yet!"
Reveller was cold all over, his ears were clammy,
but there was still a stir in his heart. They got
brandy down his throat, they rubbed him with it,
and a tremble of recognition in the eyelid answered
them.   They persevered, and in ten minutes the
patient, with a hot-water bag at his back, was warm
again and sleeping quietly. John Michael rose to
his feet and stretched himself, looking like an Italian
sailor, with his dark head, and bare, brown throat
and feet.

"I thought he was done for!" he said, shaking
down the thermometer; "it was a good thing I
was awake and heard him when he cried out."

"Go back to your bed now," said Mrs. Fitz-Symons,
looking at him with the mother's eye, that admires,
and absorbs, and embraces. "You're tired, my
child, and indeed you have a right to be tired."

"I'll stay for a while yet," he said, sitting down on
a ragged ottoman near the door; "you have the room
rather hot." He pulled the door open by the loop
of string that served as a handle. "It's not a cold
night at all."

"Well, poor Miss Rowan thought it was cold
enough," replied his mother, snatching at the topic
that was nearest her heart; "I hope she won't be the
worse of it."

"I'm afraid she won't be the better of it, anyway,"
said John Michael; "I daresay it'll be no harm for
her that she'll get no more hunting here."

His voice was of a matter-of-fact dreariness; he
had picked up an old hound-muzzle and was mechan-
ically straightening its wires with his capable fingers.

Mrs. Fitz-Symons left Reveller abruptly, and sat
down on the ottoman beside her son.

"Oh, Johnny!" she said, catching at his hand,
"my darling boy! If you leave me my heart will
break!"

She sat fondling his hand, and sniffing, and gazing

at him, afraid of him, afraid for him, a person greatly
to be pitied.

John Michael was also suffering, for her as well as
for himself, but he had no way of telling her so.

" What's the use of talking ? " he said, at last,
after one of the silences to which his mother had
learned, not without difficulty, to submit. " If the
hounds go, I've got to go too.   You heard him
saying that yourself.   If I wanted to stay he'd not
keep me."

" He's not everybody ! " flashed Mrs. Fitz-Symons.
"What does it matter what he wants !   There's others
I think more of than him want you to stay !   I know
one anyway—— "

Her son looked at her with tired, uninspired eyes.
He thought she was speaking of herself, and the
fetter of undemonstrativeness was on him.

" Ah, they'd say a good deal just to please you,"
he said, " but there's none of them will do anything.
Where would they get the money ? "

" Miss Rowan would help you," said his mother,
taking her hand off his lest he should feel how much
it trembled ; she told me so herself, and she can do
it too."

John Michael regarded his mother in almost angry
bewilderment.   He was accustomed to discount her
enthusiasms, but this amazing statement had, as it
were, to be swallowed whole.

" She doesn't understand," he said with confusion
and even indignation.   " How could we take her
money—if that's what you mean ? "

His mother's heart rose high at sight of his embarrassment, could it be ?—oh, could it be ?——

" I'd take anything from her," she said, watching
John Michael's face. " because she's a real lady, and
the nicest girl, yes—— " here Mrs. Fitz-Symons, in
the intoxication of the subject, deviated into rhap-
sody, " and the handsomest girl that ever I've met
in my life."

"Did she tell you she'd buy the pack?" said John Michael, incredulously. "Does she want to run the hounds?"

"Ah, God help you!" said Mrs. Fitz-Symons, with sudden exasperation, "she didn't say the very words. You think there's nothing in the world to think of but the hounds. No! but I'll answer for it that whatever you ask her, she'll not refuse it."

John Michael got up without making any reply and went over to the sofa where Reveller lay. He stood with his back to his mother, looking down at the sick hound in silence. Reveller acknowledged his presence with that little movement of the hind leg that was the nearest he could go to a salutation. Through the perturbation of John Michael's thoughts went the assurance that the puppy was better.

"It's nearly time for him to have something more," he said.

His mother got up and came over to him. "Ah, Johnny," she exclaimed, putting her hand on his shoulder. "What sort of a man are you at all? Isn't it plain enough what I'm telling you? Why can't you ask her to marry you? As sure as I'm standing here she'd take you. She as good as told me so!"

Her son shook her hand off, and for the first time in their joint lives he turned on her in anger.

"I'm—I'm surprised that you'd say such a thing," he hesitated and stammered, because he was not in the habit of being angry, violently angry, and, in any case, was possessed of a limited vocabulary "And to say a dirty low thing like that about a lady—"

"And what harm have I said?" interrupted his mother, stung to quick wrath. "I've said no more than what's the truth! Why shouldn't she like you? If you were any good at all you'd ask her yourself and she'd tell you fast enough!"

" Well, I won't ask her," said John Michael, as
loudly as she.

He made for the door.

" And it's a damned shame for you to talk like
that.   I don't want her any more than she wants me !
He stopped, holding the edge of the door in his hand,
with the darkness and stillness of the house before
him.   " I'd hate to be married.   I'd sooner sweep
a kennel in America ! "

The name fell like a sword, severing his life from
his mother's.

He passed out into the dark.   His room was at
the end of the passage, and he groped his way to it,
hot with anger.   Behind him, near the other end
of the passage, an intermittent flicker of firelight
showed at the crack of a door that was slightly ajar,
the spare room door, whose lock the carpenter could
not find time to repair, even under the most stimulating and exacting circumstances.

After John Michael had left her Mrs. Fitz-Symons
sat down again by the table, and was very quiet for
a few minutes, with her hand over her eyes.   Some
stir from Reveller aroused her attention ; she got up
and gave him the milk and brandy that, in their
common-place, humble, tangible way, had driven
back the King of Mystery.

Still kneeling beside Reveller, she broke down
suddenly.

" What good is it for you now to get well ? " she
cried, " my poor puppy !   My poor puppy ! "

Reveller was dully aware of warm drops falling on
his side.

CHAPTER XXVI

MRS. MASTERMAN set forth from Lake View at half-past ten o'clock next morning in a covered car, with a selection from Katharine's wardrobe, and a heart filled with legitimate indignation. Having on the previous evening endured considerable anxiety, and held back dinner until nine o'clock, and having then, as she said, fed upon cinders, the usual wrathful reaction had occurred, and she had spent what remained of the evening in formulating an ultimatum to Miss Rowan.

The covered car swung and bounced in the ruts with the unexpected levity of its race, and Katharine's dressing-box glissaded on the seat opposite to her, and smote her in the knees with human and malign intelligence at any moment that it found her off her guard. After the storm the air was keen and gay, and the sun shone sharply in the purged atmosphere. The road that she looked out upon through the black leather curtains had been scarified by flood and tempest down to its stony sole ; the loosened streams still flowed over it, and here and there men were putting sods of grass on the roofs of their houses, to act as stop-gaps where the slates had been blown away.

In Mrs. Masterman's pocket was a letter from Ulick Adare, received that morning ; an entertaining, agreeable letter, that had, nevertheless, entirely failed to entertain her. It bore the Paris postmark, and conveyed, with apparent satisfaction, the information that a man had asked him to shoot woodcock in Albania ; the man had a yacht, which was now at Genoa, and he, Ulick, was going to turn a little money by telling lies about the show for a London weekly paper. He hoped, with faultless propriety, that Miss Rowan and Dermot were enjoying themselves, and he imparted to Mrs. Masterman some of the newest side-lights upon people and politics, because, as he reminded her, she had always told him that all the scandal that was worth hearing came from men's clubs. Jean Masterman drew forth the letter, and re-read it in snatches, as the bounding of the inside car permitted, and said to herself, not for the first time, that what Katharine wanted was a good shaking. A specially exasperating feature was that she had no exact idea of how matters stood between any of them. Reserve was, no doubt, an admirable quality, theoretically, and in its proper place; but, as is not infrequent, Mrs. Masterman found that where she was concerned it was quite inappropriate.

But facts, at all events, spoke for themselves. Here was Ulick, careering to Genoa, and to Albania, a place that, as far as she was concerned existed merely to provide costumes for fancy dress balls; and here, also, was Katharine, buried in the inmost heart of the unspeakable Fitz-Symons establishment; not only ignoring its unspeableness, but probably enjoying every moment of it. At this point the covered-car pulled up with an abruptness suggestive of having banged into a wall, and through the little window in front she saw her driver descending to open the gates of Ashgrove. It gave a terrible reality to everything; it was like going to visit Katharine at her home.

" How she can think twice of that fox-hunting yokel," she thought, as the horse, and his partner and plagiarist, the inside car, cantered in unison up the narrow avenue, " whose solitary means of expression is to blow a horn ! " She was rather taken with this idea, and placed it on a mental shelf for development in her next letter to Ulick Adare. He was a person to whom it was easy to write letters ; he stimulated, and he also understood. But what a

N

score for the Fitz-Symons family! She pictured
to herself the odious sleekness of the master of the
house, the exultation of its mistress, and of John
Michael—No! it was impossible to conceive of poor
Dumb Crambo as being exultant about anything,
except, perhaps, killing a fox! She would do him
that justice. Nevertheless, he could not but perceive
the preposterous homage offered to him by that
double-dyed idiot, Katharine, and no doubt by this
time he had awakened to his opportunities.

Here the hall door was opened to her by Mary,
capless, and wearing an apron whose complexion
indicated that it had seen moving accidents by
flood and field, specially by flood. Mrs. Masterman
thought that it took its place in the general situation.
The mistress was in, Mary informed her, and Miss
Rowan was above in her room, she didn't rise out of
the bed yet. Mrs. Masterman waited in the drawing-
room, and the drawing-room, and its furniture and
adornments, seen in the cold sunlight of the December
morning, and enhanced by the first flight of Christmas cards, made the situation more crushing than
ever.

Mary returned. The mistress was very sorry,
but she was engaged for a few minutes minding the
dog.

"That's the hound that was poisoned, Ma'am,"
supplemented the envoy, and would Mrs. Masterman go up and see Miss Rowan? Mrs. Masterman,
acceded to the request, and in the hall came suddenly
face to face with John Michael; he had a bowl in
one hand, and in the other was a saucer with an egg
upon it; he looked, she thought, as if he was taking
part in a competition at a Gymkhana. In the shock of
the encounter the egg rushed round and round the
saucer as though trying to escape; a similar emotion
obviously agitated its bearer, and Jean Masterman,
unwillingly, pitied him as women were wont to pity
John Michael in social aspects.

"I'm sorry to hear that you have an invalid hound to look after," she said, with more civility than she had intended to show.

"He's a lot better to-day," stammered John Michael, backing out of her path.

"I've come to fetch Miss Rowan," continued Jean looking at him with an expression armoured with pleasantness and conventionality.

At the word the egg sprang over the edge of the saucer, and fell to the oilcloth, never to rise again.

Jean Masterman, murmuring sympathies, passed on, with darkness in her heart, her worst fears confirmed.

"Well, my dear," she began, with a well-compounded mixture of sarcasm and amusement, as she crossed the threshold of Katharine's room, "you have indeed drained the cup of pleasure to the dregs." Even as she spoke, something prostrate and beaten in Katharine's aspect startled her. "And I can't say you look as if it had agreed with you."

"I am rather tired, that's all," said Katharine, with a pale effort at defiance. She felt the tone exactly as it was intended she should feel it.

Mrs. Masterman advanced, tall and pleasing to look at in her long, fur coat, taking in Katharine with her observant, trusty eyes; the faint scent, that Katharine knew so well, conveying its wonted association as she stooped over and kissed her. As her soft cheek touched Katharine's, Jean Masterman's kindness asserted itself.

"You wretched child!" she murmured, "what have you been doing to yourself?"

Katharine was suddenly overwhelmed by a feeling that she was going to break down.

"Don't, Jean," she said, turning away her face, "don't be nice to me or, or——"

Jean Masterman made as though she had not heard. She sat down on a small and decrepit chair, of the variety that becomes decrepit in early middle life;

it gave a perceptible stagger, and Mrs. Masterman rose hastily to her feet.

" Don't tell Mrs. Fitz-Symons that I broke it ! " She sat down on the side of the bed. " This, I presume, is Mrs. Fitz-Symons' tea-gown ? " She picked up the garment in question and held it up by a voluminous and dumpy sleeve. " You wore it at dinner, no doubt ? I am sure it suited Madam to perfection ! "

While she talked she wondered what had happened. She had often seen Katharine tired, and she had once or twice seen her ill, but she had never before seen her vanquished.

" I'm quite ready to go home, you know," said Katharine, recovering herself.

" I've brought you some things," said Mrs. Masterman ; " I thought that probably neither you nor your habit would be fit for publication to-day."

" I don't think I'm going to ride again for some time," said Katharine in a level voice, " my back feels rather done for."

" Your back ? " said Mrs. Masterman, quickly. " Did you strain it yesterday ? "

" Well, not exactly," said Katharine, with hesitation it's where I felt it after that fall—as if I had a hundred-weight of lead on my shoulders."

Jean Masterman was not a woman given to the use of strong language, but in her heart she said with excommunicatory fervour, " Damn hunting ! "

To Katharine she said airily, " My good child, that doesn't surprise me in the least ! It is the result of overdoing everything, as you always do ! "

She covertly glanced at Katharine's colourless face and the darkness under her eyes.

" You weren't fit for such a long day ; no more hunting for you for the present, my young friend ! "

" You need not distress yourself about my hunting," said Katharine. " There's not going to be any more hunting here. The hounds are to be given up."

Mrs. Masterman found her exultation more difficult to conceal than the anxiety that it overlaid.

"When was that decided on ? " she asked.

" Last night, I believe," said Katharine, restlessly sweeping back the hair from her forehead. " There has been poisoning—and rows—it's a long story——"

" Rather a blow for this establishment, isn't it ? " said Jean Masterman, moving towards the window, and idly noting a dingy old hound, standing on three legs and scratching its ribs with the fourth. " I can imagine that the senior partner will survive it, but what will the junior member of the firm think of it ! "

" He's going to America," said Katharine.

In her surprise, and, it must be added, her heartfelt satisfaction, Mrs. Masterman turned and looked at Katharine. She saw a slow tide of colour creep gradually up her face till it met the bright wing of hair that lay on her forehead. " Oh, my poor Katharine ! " she thought, with a pang of dismay ; " can it possibly be as bad as that ! "

Then her own ineradicable point of view asserted itself in her mind. She thought of Adare's letter in her pocket, and said to herself :

" Whatever her method may be, she certainly has the gift of scattering them."

CHAPTER XXVII

MRS. DELANTY, as was frequently the case, was not pleased with old Mahony, the smith, and early on the morning following the hunt, she proceeded to the forge on her bicycle with the intention of telling him so.

She was now standing in the doorway of the forge

watching, with alert eyes, the operation of shoeing her bay mare.

" Now, Mahony," she said sharply, " put down that rasp. The mare's feet are well enough as God made them."

" I'm thinking there wasn't much talk of hunting-shoes that time," said the smith, flinging down the rasp, " a quare way you'd look at me when she was after coming in with an over-reach ! "

" That's no reason you should take the toes off her ! " returned the widow, breaking with zest the accustomed spear with old Mahony, " and mind now you don't go squeezing her heels. I declare there isn't one of you smiths but would give a horse a foot like a mule for the sake of three ha'porth of iron ! Look at the show you made of her the last time you shod her ! "

" Sure, my God, ma'am, it wasn't myself shod her at all last month," replied the smith, indignantly, looking up at her over the enormous horn-rimmed spectacles that he wore. " It was Willy here med them shoes." 'Twas that was the time I had the 'fluenzy. I hadn't the first shoe of them fairly made when I felt me heart scattering in me body with the wakeness. Captain Bolger was looking at me the same time. ' Throw the shoe from you,' says he, ' and go home,' says he ; ' take all that's in the house and put it on you,' says he, ' you're sick,' says he ' and dam sick ! ' I wrought in the bed for three days, and I declare to you, afther leaving the bed, if it was no more than the frivolity of putting on me little gansey, I'd be in a passpira-tion with the dint of it."

" You must have been in a poor way enough," commented Mrs. Delanty, politely. " Well ! we'll say no more about Willy's shoes, but be careful now and don't put a mule's foot on her to-day."

Old Mahony advanced to the hearth. " Fire, boy ! " he commanded his acolyte, thrusting into the reddening cinders the shoe that he had been fitting.

"By all I can hear," he resumed, "a mule might be able for as much hunting as there'll be in the country from this out."

Mrs. Delanty laughed lightly. "You're a great man to get the news, Mahony. But maybe you didn't get the whole of it this time."

"Maybe not indeed," returned Mahony, with his air of the wearied philosopher. I got as much as I wanted anyway. It's bad news for a smith when hounds go out of the country."

"Who told you they were going out of the country?" said Mrs. Delanty, leaning easily against the door-post, her hands in her coat pockets, and her hair a little blown by the wind over her white forehead. Her eyes were full of mischief and superior know-ledge; she thought it would do old Mahony no harm to get a bit of a fright.

"What'll you smiths, and the farmers, do when we're all driving motor-cars?" she said, with her staccato accent at its pertest and most flippant. "I suppose you'll tell me you'll have the Old Age Pension! Maybe you have it this minute!"

"Why then there's plenty that has it that wants it less," returned Mahony, quite unmoved by the reflection upon his age, "and I might have as good a right to it as some of them! There was a man told me he was after getting it, and he no more than the one age with meself. What did he do but to get an owld Alibi down from the mountain, and himself went away out of the place for that day."

"I suppose he had good friends on the Commit-tee?" said the widow, affably.

The bay mare was tired and drowsy, and her head had nodded to her knees; she lifted it suddenly and pricked her ears. Mrs. Delanty glanced up the road and saw a couple of horses coming towards her down the hill. Tom Coyne was riding one and leading the other, the grey mare who had so casually and so effectively made her entrance into Katharine's career.

Tom Coyne was very silent. He did not attempt to meet Mrs. Delanty's skilled and highly critical observations on his horses ; he did not even try to explain how he had missed the finish of the run. Mrs. Delanty decided that he was in low spirits about the hounds, and made up her mind that Gus had probably given him "the sack," and that she would make Fanshawe take him on.

The old smith regarded him darkly from under his grey eyebrows, said conventionally that it was a fine day, and went on fashioning in silence the shoe for the bay mare. Under the disastrous circumstances good breeding forbade that he should be the first to open the topic that was uppermost in interest. Moreover, such a matter as the poisoning of hounds was one to be approached with caution, especially in mixed company. It belonged to the neither side of things, a side with ramifications fraught with possible danger, and not one to be lightly introduced by a servant of the public.

"How is Reveller to-day, Tom ? " went on Mrs. Delanty. "I hope you're going to pull him through?"

" He's nearly better ; I think he'll do now, Ma'am," returned Tom Coyne, listlessly.

"Ah, poor Sindbad and Fantasy ! " said Mrs. Delanty. "I was sorry to my heart for them. There was nothing could be done for them. I saw that from the first. Mr. Fanshawe wanted to gallop for Mr. Jagoe, but I told him there wasn't a vet. in Ireland that could save them. Brieshka didn't spare the strychnine."

" That the divil in hell mightn't spare fire to him," said Tom Coyne, with intense concentration, as he adjusted his stirrup leather.

The smith, with the mare's hind foot in his lap and his mouth full of nails, muttered something that might or might not have been " Amen."

" The Master is after summonsing him for an assault," went on Tom Coyne, " but what good is that when they're all to be done away with ? Master Johnny was going round them in the kennels with me this morning. ' Toom,' he says, ' I'll never throw them into a covert again,' and the tears rained from his eyes."

" No blame to him " said the smith.

A quick moisture of sympathy shone in Mrs. Delanty's dark eyes.

" They're not gone yet, Tom," she said hastily, with her emotion in her voice ; " he might show us sport with them yet."

" He'll show no more sport in this country," said Tom Coyne heavily, yet upheld by the greatness of his tidings. " He's after telling me he's going to America."

The nails dropped from the smith's mouth, and Mrs. Delanty's groom, hitherto silent in the numbing presence of his mistress, said, " For God's sake ! "

The remarkable thing was that Mrs. Delanty said nothing. With one hand on the door-post she stared at Tom Coyne, with her lips parted and her delicate brows knitted as if in the effort to comprehend.

The smith took up his parable. " As nice a young man, and as dacent a young man as ever stood in the Barony. There wasn't one in the country but had a good word for him. I knew him since he was the height o' me hammer, puckin' round the counthry on a dunky, and I knew his father before him ; I'm shoeing horses for them, seed and breed, for fifty year, and I declare to God, if I had a silver shoe in my hand, I wouldn't grudge it to put it on his mare this minute."

To this obituary oration Tom Coyne listened in dignified acquiescence, as became a representative of the family, besides which, the fixity of Mrs. Delanty's gaze at him was attracting his attention.

" Do you say he told you he was going to America ?"

she asked, in a voice that seemed to be drained dry,
like a little roadside rivulet in drought.

"He did, ma'am. He said he had a situation
offered him there, and he'd be out of this in a month."

Tom Coyne felt that the zenith of tidings had been
attained, and artistically ceased.

Mrs. Delanty was silent, but Tom Coyne knew
that his news had had a reception worthy of its magnitude.

Mrs. Delanty took her bicycle from where it leaned
against the white-washed wall of the forge, and
walked away rapidly up the hill, wheeling it beside
her, in the opposite direction from her home. Her
stable-boy, Danny, went to the door of the forge
and watched her.

The smith said in a low voice to Tom Coyne, "That
hit her, begob."

"She had a wish for him always," returned Tom
Coyne in a swift whisper.

Danny came back from his observations. "It's
the turn for Ashgrove she's taken," he said with
some excitement.

The smith disliked all stable-boys on principle.

"Throw me here that rasp," he said, repressively,
and proceeded, as it were absently, to use it on the
mare's hind foot.

Mrs. Delanty walked fast up the hill, because the
shock was driving her before it. The December sunshine struck her cheek with a faint warmth, and cast
her trim shadow before her on the road. Johnny
was going, Johnny was leaving the country! It was
as though a clanging bell were telling her this incessantly, hammering it in, banging it in. Why
should he go away because a couple of hounds were
poisoned? Tom Coyne said he had got a situation
in America; why couldn't he get a situation here?
Was it something about Miss Rowan?

Here she turned up the by-road that was the short
way to Ashgrove, a bad road for a bicycle, as she

well knew, but it would be better further on. She
must see Johnny at once, before he went on with
this mad plan of going away to America. Had Miss
Rowan refused him ? Was that why he was going ?
No ! she hadn't done that ! It was enough to have
seen her face last night, when they were at tea together in that cottage, to know that she was only
ready to jump at him. With her money and all,
he wouldn't be bothered with that big lump of a
Scotchwoman, or whatever she was ! He'd sooner
go to America !

Then Johnny's eyes when they had met hers, and
she was telling him about the poison. He had not
looked at her like that, like a hurt child that wanted
her to help him, since the day that his mare broke
her back jumping at the Agricultural Show, and she
had run back into the town for the gun for the vet.
to shoot her with. They were great friends after
that. That was the first autumn after she came to
the country, and she used to get up early and go out
cubbing with him, and he told her once she was the
only lady he ever knew he'd trust to watch the end
of a covert. It was his old mother that interfered
that time, and frightened him ; she knew that very
well. She could have had Gus, too, hopping, that
first year ; she wished she had, if it was only to spite
the mother ; it was she put Gus against her too.
Well—Johnny wouldn't stay at home now to please
his mother. She found that some tears were running
down her face ; the knot tightened in her throat.
Maybe—she stood still—maybe she herself had something to say to him that would make him change
his mind !

She leaned heavily upon her bicycle ; it had been
heavy work pushing it up the steep lane. She had
excellent wind (though her friends were wont to put
up their eyebrows about the smallness of her waist),
but her breath was coming hard and short. The
lane had carried her high along the hillside (that hill

from which Katharine had seen the spike of File-na-Showk), and up there in the sunshine with the thin wind snatching at her hair and cooling her hot face, she herself was lifted above her little life of calculations and economies. Her resolve gathered strength ; the thing that might be, became the thing that should be.

She had turned from the lane, and its stones and water-courses, into one of the old " Famine Roads," made to give employment, not to be employed ; the grass that covered it was short and smooth ; there were no ruts in it, nothing except the fresh hoofmarks of the two Ashgrove horses. She mounted her bicycle and rode on determinedly against the gradual upward slope. She must get back again in time for lunch. Fanshawe would be arriving, and if she were not back to meet him, Janetta would have a fit. Fanshawe's face rose before her; his slow, amorous gazes, his large, stupid nose, his amiable, babyish mouth. She suddenly felt as if she could not stand Fanshawe. She was tired of him and his love-making ; more than that, she was beginning to suspect him of a precocious capacity in the matter of not committing himself.

" All men are like that, old or young ! " she thought angrily, " carry on as long and as far as you'll let them, and then away with them ! He'll find that that may do for some, but it'll not do for me ! "

She was up on the ridge of the hill now ; the last pinch had been steep, and she got off her bicycle to rest for a moment. Below her were the trees of Ashgrove, brown and purple among the pale meadows. Nearer to her than they were, stretched the long red roof of the kennels ; she could see the kennel-yards, she could even see in them the white specks that were the hounds, lying out in the sun. A thin blue smoke, coming from the chimney, created its inevitable effect of tranquility. For her, the familiar picture shook in the tremor of her purpose.

On the grassy track in front of her lay a drift of
white feathers, telling where Dan Russel the Fox
had yet again, in his masterful way, left his mark
upon the lives of others.

CHAPTER XXVIII

JOHN MICHAEL had been very angry with his
mother, and his wrath still simmered, like the
porridge that he was stirring. He was standing on a box beside the kennel-boiler, slowly and
strenuously working a long-handled shovel round
and round in the thick, sallow mass that steamed
and seethed, and heaved up sluggish bubbles that
swelled and broke with a sound like the gabbling and
chuckling of fat people. He was angry with his
mother because she had said what she had no right
to say about Miss Rowan ; rotten nonsense, he sum-
marised it, as he levered the shovel round against
the edge of the boiler ; he was also angry with her
because she was ever and always bothering the life
out of him about getting married. Well—she
wouldn't be able to bother him long. That was the
worst of it. John Michael loved his mother, not as
much as she loved him, for there is no son living who
loves his mother as he is loved by her ; but she com-
prised for him the world of home and affection, and
he hated leaving her. Besides he knew, and no one
except herself knew better than he, what his going
away would mean to her.

It hurt very badly, as he thought of it with the
compassion that is part of the son's love, because he
knows his mother's need to be greater than his own,
but everything hurt to-day. The face of old Rachel,
as she had looked up at him that morning, with the

beautiful glance of confidence and adoration that only a dog can give ; Lottery's long chestnut nose, with its crooked blaze, over the stable door, as she banged at it with her knee in demand for his attention, tired and all as she was, he thought, after her big day ; even the lamentations of the kennel-boys' mother, delivered to him through the bars of the kennel-yard, were all foretastes of what good-bye was going to be. He stirred harder than ever, and braced himself with the thought of escape from Gus. Gus had said things to him last night that no one could stand. John Michael was a pacific fellow, not given to resentment, or perceptive of affronts, but when a quiet nature is wounded it is not easily healed.

A hound or two bayed languidly and fretfully in the yard, there was a light step outside, and the low doorway of the feeding house was darkened. John Michael looked down from his perch beside the boiler, and saw Mrs. Delanty standing there.

" Good morning, Johnny," she said, and it struck him that she must have come fast, because she seemed to be out of breath. " I wanted to know how Reveller was, and I just bicycled over."

" Thank you very much," said John Michael, gratefully, " I think he's all right. He was near dying last night, but we got at him in time."

He continued his laborious circuiting of the boiler with the shovel, as he spoke ; his coat was off and his shirt sleeves were rolled up; the action of his arms and shoulders was rhythmic and powerful, and strangely graceful."

" You'll excuse me going on with the pudding, it's just finished."

" Well, thank goodness, we saved him anyway ! " said Mrs. Delanty, moving a step forward and looking up at him. " I was doctoring at him for half an hour yesterday morning."

" I'm greatly obliged to you for what you did," he

said, stopping for a moment and leaning on the handle of his stirrer; "only for you he was lost."

As she looked up at him he saw that her face was white and her eyes were shining.

"Johnny," she said hurriedly, "is it possible that it's true what I hear, that you're going to America?"

"It's true right enough," he said shortly. He descended from the box, and proceeded to rake out what was left of the fire, with his usual thoroughness and attention to detail. "I don't want the pudding to burn," he said apologetically.

She waited until he had finished, enduring the noise and the delay as best she might. "Johnny," she began again, speaking rapidly and jerkily, "I know for a fact that Basil Fanshawe's going to buy the hounds——"

John Michael looked at her quickly. "Well, so he can," he said, after a moment's pause. "It's the first I heard of it."

"I'm the only one that knows it," said the widow, displaying through all the stress of emotion her sense of commanding importance, "and you're the only one that I've told it to."

"It'd be more use to tell it to Gus," said John Michael, ignoring the compliment, "they're his hounds."

"Sure, of course, I know Gus will sell them to him, and be only delighted," said the widow, impatiently.

She came nearer to him. "But what would hounds be in this country without you, Johnny?"

John Michael recoiled almost visibly before the personal appeal.

"Fanshawe can get plenty of huntsmen as good as me and better," he said.

"That's a lie, and you know it!" said the widow, vehemently. "It's you he wants, and no one else!"

John Michael's heart gave a throb or two, but he maintained a steadfast countenance. Suspicion, reasonless and deep, like that of a woodland animal kept him silent.

"I told him he'd never get on with the people here without you, let alone the hunting itself; you may be sure I made him understand that," went on Mrs. Delanty, erecting as it were the dais on which she would present herself to John Michael as his patron-saint.

He did not answer at first; he could make an instant decision on a rough hillside, with hounds at fault, and the Field in twenty wrong places at once, but in the ordinary affairs of life his mind moved slowly and without self-reliance.

"Did he ask you to speak to me?" he said at length.

"He—he didn't exactly say the word—we were talking the whole thing over, riding home last night. He was asking my advice; he was only anxious to do whatever I suggested——" She looked at him as if her caressing eyes should complete her meaning. "I will do anything for you, and he will do anything for me," was what they tried to say.

John Michael slowly and deliberately laid down the iron rod with which he had been raking out his fire.

"I'd sooner he'd speak to me himself," he said uncomfortably.

"It's the same thing," she broke in, putting her shaking hand on the edge of the cooler to steady herself, "he'll do whatever I say—you'll be as good as your own master, and you'll get a good screw into the bargain! I'll see to that! Oh, Johnny! You mustn't go! You and me would run the whole show between us!"

Her cheeks were hot and her voice was changed and wavering.

"It'd be like old times when we were friends first!"

John Michael was aware of a pang approaching to physical terror, and, by some sub-connection of

ideas, saw before his eyes an ornate cigarette case,
bestowed upon him four Christmases ago by Mrs.
Delanty, and never since revealed to human eye, an
object at once abhorrent and alarming to him.

"Thank you," he said hurriedly, "I don't think that
would do very well." He understood with sudden
illumination what it would mean. Lily Delanty to
boss the hounds. Lily Delanty to arrange the meet,
to say Go here, or Go there, or even Go home!
"Thank you," he repeated, "I think I'd do better to
go to America." He held his head back, with his
chin in the air, like a shy, handsome schoolboy,
and turned half away from her.

She suddenly caught his arm with both her hands,
and put her hot forehead against his shoulder.

"Johnny!" she cried, beginning to sob, "wouldn't
you stay for my sake? Don't you know how fond
I am of you?"

What more she said neither she nor John Michael
can ever clearly remember, nor do they desire to do
so, but in that insane moment of surrender and self-
forgetfulness, the small, second-rate, egotistical soul
of Mrs. Delanty found wings, and spread them in
larger air.

It was over in an instant, and she knew that she
had failed, that she had given herself away for nothing.
They were standing opposite to each other in suffo-
cating tension and embarrassment. The widow
was the first to pull herself together.

"You needn't look so frightened!" she said, in
furious sarcasm, dashing away her tears, "I'm
going!"

He stood motionless, till the beat of her speeding
step had died. Then, with weakened knees, he
feebly scrambled on to the box by the boiler and
picked up the shovel again. The boiler was still
very hot, and the "pudding" was in need of being
stirred.

"Oh, my goodness!" said this serious and un-

U

sentimental son of the South-west, as he painstakingly dragged the shovel round and round. " That was awful ! "

CHAPTER XXIX

MISS JANETTA SCANLAN'S best dress was by no means what it had been at the beginning of the hunting season. Luncheons, teas, even dinners, had exacted its appearance with a frequency undreamed of during any of its previous incarnations ; (the first of which, it may not be out of place to mention, had been at the funeral of her late brother-in-law, Delanty). She liked Mr. Fanshawe, who had now arrived at the stage of calling her " Miss Janetta," and of chaffing her heavily, and with enormous success ; but when it came to playing the dual part of cook and chaperon three times a week, and more, she said to herself that Lily was spending a deal too much on him, and that the butcher's book was a " fright." None the less she continued, unmurmuringly, unquestioning, to prepare repasts for him, nor did it seem remarkable to her to spend her mornings in concocting and setting forth savoury meats, that were eaten without comment, before her anxious eyes, in less than five minutes.

She was sitting in the kitchen on the morning after the hunt, trying to extract counsel and comfort from an erudite article on " Lady-like Luncheons " in a weekly paper when Kate entered with an egg in her hand.

" That's all that's in it, Miss, and where was it only within in the donkey's house ! I got it inside in the major. How cozy she laid it there the way I wouldn't get it ! "

" It was the grey hen, I suppose," said Miss
Janetta, abstractedly ; she knew that Kate was
alluding to the manger, but what " Maitre d'hôtel "
might mean was a problem beyond her. Lily would
know.

" Is the mistress outside ? " she asked. " Did
she come back from the forge yet ? "

" She did not, Miss," said Kate.

" Bother her ! " replied Miss Janetta, abandoning
the Lady-like Luncheon and falling back upon
cutlets.

It was then twelve o'clock ; in the small yet
critical labours of the kitchen the time passed swiftly,
each minute more piercingly flavoured by the naked
and repellent raw onion. Miss Scanlan had arrived
at the stage of cutting out paper frills for the cutlets,
as if she were making clothes for a doll, when the
well-known drumming of the motor smote upon her
ear.

" Well, never welcome him ! " said Miss Janetta,
" and me not dressed ! Under heaven what's keeping Lily I don't know ! "

Fanshawe sat alone in the drawing-room and
tried to be patient. The little room was very
familiar to him now, and in itself, with its tender
memories of cigarettes over the fire, and of *tête-à-
tête* hunting-teas, it gave him a sense of ease and of
welcome, and even of home. He sprawled in the
chair that he now looked upon as his own, and
stretched his long legs towards the fender, and
studied the dramatically wistful photograph of Mrs.
Delanty in evening dress, that stood on the table
beside him. He mused over the depth of her eyes,
he lingered over the soft line of her throat, he smiled
to himself in adoration of the delicate droop of the
lips that chaffed him, that were gracious to him,
but that had always, hitherto, been unattainable.

He felt very much in love, and strode to the
window, and stared down towards the white gate to

catch the first glimpse of her, and thought that it was heartless of her to be out, when she knew he was coming over and had so much to say to her. Hang it ! if he only knew where she was he'd go and meet her. He walked back to the fireplace and regarded the photograph of the late Delanty that hung in the place of honour over the chimneypiece. He had many times regarded it with dislike and curiosity, and he thought, as he had often thought before, that he looked like a fat actor, and remembered how old Bolger, in answer to his enquiries, had described Mr. Delanty's appearance as "a cross between an undertaker and a chimney-sweep, with a dash of the corner-boy thrown in." What a champion rouser he must have been ! But how could *she* know—she was only seventeen when she married him, poor little girl !

Here Miss Janetta entered in the black silk, whose rustle was not what it had been on the day that it had lent dignity to the obsequies of the champion rouser.

" Lily hasn't come in yet," she began, very apologetically ; she was accustomed to finding herself a disappointment. " Danny's after coming back from the forge. He says she went over the hill with her bike to Ashgrove. It must be she got some message from Tom Coyne. Danny says he was at the forge."

" Gone to Ashgrove ! " repeated Fanshawe, with surprise and obvious offence. " Why, I was going to take her there this afternoon ! "

" It might be it was something about the poor dog that got the poison," suggested Miss Janetta, with every wish to be consolatory.

Fanshawe's face flushed. " I think Fitz-Symons might look after his own hounds," he said huffily. He hesitated. " If you don't mind, Miss Janetta, I think I'll just walk up the road and meet her."

" Do now, do ! " said Miss Janetta, eagerly. The bang of the hall door was music to her ear.

She would have time now to put a few Christmas
roses on the dinner-table. It really was a great
shame for Lily to keep that poor young man waiting
on her this way. Any resentment on her own behalf
never occurred to Miss Janetta's humble mind.

Fanshawe's long legs took him up the road at a
very considerable pace. No doubt that was what
was keeping her, he said to himself, she had been sent
for to doctor the hound. Infernal cheek he called
it. They knew jolly well she was cleverer than the
whole lot of them put together. Then he thought
of last night, at the cottage where they had had tea.
He remembered how she and John Michael had said
awfully intimate sort of things to each other at the
door, things he couldn't hear. He hadn't liked it
at the time, and he liked it less now that he thought
about it. He had always had a notion that there
had been something between them once, and old
Bolger had hinted something about it too. He had
tried to pin her about it one afternoon coming home
from hunting, and she didn't altogether deny it.
She just rotted and humbugged about it, as she
always did. Anyhow he wasn't going to stand her
being ordered about like this.

He passed the forge at a good four miles an hour,
and took the turn up the hill that Mrs. Delanty had
taken in the morning. He went up it, as she had
gone up it before him, with his own thought, like
Sir Bedivere's, driving him like a goad, even as she
had been driven. Such a road for a bicycle! he
thought, fuming; it was just like her, though, not
to think about that where a hound was concerned.

He turned a corner in the lane, and saw, up the
hill ahead of him, a bicycle lying on the ground, and
a little figure huddled against the bank near it.

Mrs. Delanty heard his running step, and raised
her head from her hands. She and the bicycle
had come down with some force; she was covered
with mud, she had hurt her elbow, and one hand

was badly scraped. Nothing very serious, but it
had shaken her, and she had lain there against the
bank, and felt that the courage was out of her. She
had felt bad enough before it happened, she had
said to herself, and now she didn't care if she lay
there all day.

As she tried to struggle to her feet, Fanshawe's
arms were round her, supporting her, protecting her,
making a shelter for her. She felt suddenly that
he was a man, a big stalwart creature, that he loved
her, that he wanted her.

"I was coming too fast down the hill," she said,
shaking all over, as she leaned against him, and felt
the comfort of his support; "I knew I was keeping
you waiting."

"You were hurrying on my account!" whispered
Fanshawe, pressing her to him.

How slight and small she was in his arms! How
fragile! Such a little thing! How white and tear-
stained her face was as he looked down into it!

"You shall never go away from me again!" he
said, dizzily, as the lips that had been unattainable
were his at last.

CHAPTER XXX

KATHARINE sat in the garden of the Hotel
Beau Séjour, and looked down upon the
radiant Bay of Liguria. It was April, and the air was
warm and rich; carnations and freesias, and roses
gave of their best to it, the scent of hot pine-trees
was in it, and the immeasurable blueness of the
Mediterranean came up with it through the cloistral
grey of the olives. It was very quiet in the garden;
somewhere near, a little fountain of a single thread

made a stealthy sound, like a whisper, or the stealing
footstep of a nymph.   Far below, in the cove, a
wind that Katharine could hear but could not feel,
was driving green wavelets on to the rocks, white-
hooded, and hissing like snakes.   It was St. George's
Day, and at intervals the bells of San Giorgio, down
in the Port below the olive woods, broke into a dance
in honour of their patron.

Katharine looked across the bay to the long coast
of Southern Italy, where the white houses of Chiavari
and Sestri Levante crowded up from the sea, and lay
scattered like sheep on the hill-sides.   She was paler
and thinner than she had been, and something of
the assertive vigour was gone, that touch of " the
imperial votaress " that Ulick Adare had commented
on, not without asperity, a little less than a year ago.
Her grey eyes seemed larger, and more deeply set,
but the adventureousness that was native to them
was alight, as they absorbed the far beauty of the
Apennines.   This was Italy, the Italy of the Cæsars,
Italy of the Battles, of the Arts, of the people who
made the world !   She fired at the thought of what
that thick-set, truculent, old Castello, on the hill
opposite, had seen in its day.   Cœur de Lion's
galleys had steered into this very port, just as that
yacht was coming in now, leaning her white side on
the blue-green water, with her sails full and ruffling,
like the plumage of an angry swan.   She was flying
the English flag, too !   Katharine discovered at this
point that she was a little vague on the subject of
Cœur de Lion's flag, and fell to wondering if the
women in the Place had made him buy lace for
Berengaria.   She thought that if they were as determined as their descendants, they had most certainly
done so.   She speculated on how long he had taken
to get here from England, and why he had ever left
this lovely land to go back there.

" I suppose he went back for the hunting ! " she
thought ;   " as I shall ! "

She had been for three months on the southern side of the Alps, wandering with Jean Masterman (marvellously emancipated from the Nursery and Mademoiselle), and England existed only as a place on the map, that sent forth newspapers, and five-pound notes in registered envelopes. As for Ireland, Ireland was a tradition, a grey spot astray upon a misty ocean. In a remote past things had happened there ; she thought of them as little as possible, but sometimes they sprang upon her unawares, and made her understand that we may regret our sins, but we agonise over our follies. Well, Dermot was not a folly, her " Dermot, dear and brown," for whose board and lodging she was even now paying Mrs. Fanshawe. At all events she could think of Dermot without writhing, even, if that last doctor at Nice was to be believed, with visions that made her heart gallop, of his future prowess in an English country.

She looked down at the yellow hotel with the green shutters. It had taken all her strength to walk from it up the steep and stony paths to where she was sitting, and she had sunk upon the garden bench exhausted and had quoted to herself Queen Katharine's line, " My legs, like loaded branches, bow to the earth " Hunting was still a long way off; it was not good to think of it. She could see the window of her room, in which at this moment the housemaids, Gina and Francesca, obviously bored with the dull routine of household tasks, were lolling on their elbows and talking loudly and jovially. But they also reminded her of Ireland.

She closed her eyes, and through the gay voices heard the smooth rattle of a chain running out, as the English yacht came to anchor under the old Castello.

In the room next to that in which Gina and Francesca held converse Jean Masterman was writing, as a good wife should, to her husband.

" This place is excellent for Katharine, so dull

and so romantic. Ulick says he is making his obliging friend bring the yacht round here from Genoa. I don't quite know what the position is with regard to him, but I suppose it will be my duty to devote myself to the obliging friend. To tell you the truth, I shall be rather surprised if she marries any one, and whether she marries or whether she doesn't marry, she will probably be sorry for it occasionally. As for that ridiculous Dumb Crambo business, I heard rather a nice story the other day that about expresses it. Some woman saw her very respectable married butler kissing her equally respectable maid in the garden. She thought it her duty to administer a rebuke.

"' Say no more about it, my lady,' the butler said magnificently, ' it was just a freak!' "

WYMAN & SONS LTD., PRINTERS, READING AND LONDON

METHUEN'S POPULAR NOVELS

Crown 8vo. **6s. each.**

SPRING, 1913

THE LOVE PIRATE. By C. N. and A. M. WILLIAMSON, Authors of 'The Heather Moon.'

The Princess di Sereno beautiful and young, sails for America to visit California. No sooner does she reach New York than she is plunged into an adventure of which Nick Hilliard, a young Californian, is the hero. All unconsciously she becomes the 'love pirate' who takes Hilliard from the Spanish woman who adores him. The hero conducts the heroine through exciting adventures, and a drama of love and jealousy, set in the midst of California's most magnificent scenery, leads at length to a happy ending.

A KNIGHT OF SPAIN. By MARJORIE BOWEN, Author of 'I Will Maintain.'

This story is laid in the stormy and sombre last half of the sixteenth century, and deals with the fortunes of the Royal House of Spain, the most powerful, cruel, and tragic dynasty of modern Europe. The hero is Charles v's son, the gay, handsome, and heroic Don Juan of Austria, who rose to an unparalleled renown in Christendom. The story embraces the greater part of this Prince's short life, which was one glowing romance of love and war, played in the various splendours of Spain, Genoa, Venice, Naples, Sicily, Africa, Paris, and Brussels.

THE ADVENTURES OF DR. WHITTY. By GEORGE A. BIRMINGHAM, Author of 'Spanish Gold.'

Dr. Whitty is a person of some importance in the town of Ballintra, which is situated in western Connacht. He lives on the best of terms with Colonel Beresford, the local landlord, Mr. Jackson, the rector, and Father Henaghan, the parish priest. In his efforts to benefit the town, to help those in any kind of difficulty and to purify the public life of the place, he meets with a series of adventures of an unusual and amusing kind.

AN AFFAIR OF STATE. By J. C. SNAITH, Author of 'The Principal Girl,' etc.

A story which attempts to forecast the course of events in the political world in the near future. Industrial unrest, fomented by class hatred, causes a chasm to open in the life of a nation. Labour and Capital are ranged on opposite sides of an unbridgable gulf; the monarchy is imperilled and civil war imminent. This engrossing novel tells how the situation is saved by the courage and wisdom of a great man.

MARY ALL-ALONE. By JOHN OXENHAM, Author of 'The Quest of the Golden Rose.'

Mary All-Alone is the story of a girl of position and culture flung suddenly on the swirling tide of life, with no special training or aptitude for earning her living in any capacity. Her very attractiveness raises barriers against her, and her courage is strained to breaking point at times to withstand the temptations of the primrose way which would provide for her bodily comfort at the expense of her higher nature.

THE BELOVED ENEMY. By E. MARIA ALBANESI, Author of 'Olivia Mary.'

In Madame Albanesi's new story she gives a study of two temperaments, one, strong and rough, made unduly bitter by strange circumstances, yet capable of splendid qualities, and the other, a sunny-hearted girl who from being rather feather-brained impulsive, and even heartless, develops gradually into a woman of strong feelings fine courage and very real sympathy. The book deals with a love story set in rather romantic fashion.

THE PEARL-STRINGER. By PEGGY WEBLING, Author of 'A Spirit of Mirth.'

The Pearl-Stringer is a story of modern life in London. It principally deals, as the title implies, with the work and experiences of a girl who strings pearls. This is a little-known occupation, and every detail of the captivating work, is given in Miss Webling's new novel interwoven with a story of love and friendship. It is a book of many characters, quaint descriptions, and intimate talks.

THE FOOL IN CHRIST, EMANUEL QUINT. By GERHART HAUPTMANN. Translated by THOMAS SELTZER.

A translation of the most remarkable of the novels of Gerhart Hauptmann to whom the Nobel Prize for Literature in 1912 was awarded. This work attempts to place the living human Christ before sophisticated twentieth-century eyes. Whatever other effect it may have, the book cannot fail to cause discussion. In Quint, a figure at once pathetic and inspiring, the author has drawn a character whose divine charm should be felt by every reader.

CHANGE OF CLIMATE. By A. A. METHLEY, Author of 'The Key of Life.'

The twelve stories in this book, the scene of which is laid in Egypt, deal entirely with the life of the tourists and English residents in that alluring country, and illustrate some of the curious influences which change of climate and of surroundings may have on different characters and temperaments.

METHUEN'S POPULAR NOVELS—*continued.*

THE TERRORS, AND OTHER STORIES. By ARCHIBALD MARSHALL.

The stories in this book are the pick of those which Mr. Marshall has written during the past seventeen years, and they form the first collection of the kind that he has made. For the most part they take a humorous view of life and its episodes.

IF IT PLEASE YOU. By RICHARD MARSH, Author of 'Judith Lee.'

If it please you—If, Sirs and Ladies, you will do yourselves the service to glance within—here's all sorts for you. A collection as odd, as whimsical, as wonderful—may we say as humorous?—as you may be pleased to want. Here's something to each special taste; for all Honourable People, a perfect feast—If It Please You!

LED INTO THE WILDERNESS. By WILLIAM E. BAILEY.

John Martin, the hero of this story, is a missionary in a rarely visited island in the East. Here he is 'tempted of the devil' and falls. First he yields to a craving for drink, and then to allurements of another kind in the person of a beautiful half-caste girl. Her dramatic death seems to him God's punishment for his offences and he thinks he has sinned beyond redemption. His despair touches the verge of madness, but in the end he finds faith and peace.

WO₂. By MAURICE DRAKE.

This is a sensational and exciting story of present-day illicit seafaring. To explain the character of the forbidden trade would be to tell too much. Enough that International politics are concerned, and that such adventures occur as have made the fortune of earlier romances.

REQUITAL. By Mrs. J. O. ARNOLD, Author of 'The Fiddler.'

The prologue to this new novel describes how John Alderson saves the life of his friend Dacre during an ornithological expedition in Siberia. The story opens several years later when Sir Henry Dacre (now an elderly man) and Jack Alderson, son of his former rescuer are in love with the same woman, Beatrice Wylde. She marries the ornithologist, with the result that complications ensue. The scene is laid chiefly near the city of steel, Greytown.

THE EVOLUTION OF EVE. By Bertha Shelley,
Author of ' Enderby.'

In her new novel, Bertha Shelley has written emphatically a love story. It is a novel that goes straight to the heart of the reader and grips it until the very last page. The action of the story begins in Australia, but continues in London, and an effective contrast is made between the heroine's early life, with its open and rough surroundings, and the more complex environment of the somewhat raffish society in London into which she is thrown.

HADOW OF 'SHAWS. By Theo Douglas (Mrs. H. D. Everett).

The story of an unwilling wife, and her endeavour to escape the obligation of a nominal marriage, into which she was forced at the age of sixteen. When the story opens, the dreaded husband is returning from India after an absence of four years. The expedient to which she resorts, and its after consequences, supply the thread of a briskly moving romance. The scene is laid in a country village, not far remote from the London of 1796.

STUDIES IN LOVE AND IN TERROR. By Mrs. Belloc Lowndes.

Mrs. Belloc Lowndes is famous for her short stories, and this volume, which contains much matter of an exciting nature, should interest all her readers.

UNCONVENTIONAL MOLLY. By Joseph Adams, Author of ' Ten Thousand Miles through Canada.'

Unconventional Molly is an Irish romance. The heroine is a link between high life with its prejudices, and lowly life with its struggles. The destiny of the characters is worked out in an atmosphere where love and jealousy, tragedy and comedy, are brought into play. The setting of the story is on the shores of the most beautiful bay in the West.

THE WARE CASE. By George Pleydell.

In *The Ware Case* Mr. George Pleydell tells the story of a crime and its gradual unravelment. The central figures are Lady Ware, a beautiful, young, and well-bred woman, torn between deep passion and high ideals, and her pleasure-loving, shallow husband. A mysterious murder and its consequences hurl the woman into the overwhelming drama of life. The book is remarkable not only for its unfailing and intense dramatic interest, but its being a detective story about persons in whom one can believe.

PASSIONS OF STRAW. By Evelyn F. Heywood.

This story unfolds the poignant tragedy of a woman who, proud, beautiful, ambitious, finds herself wedded to a cynic and a roué. This man having shattered her happiness finally succeeds in drawing their only child into the whirlpool of his idle, vicious life. The detail of the boy's rescue by the Machiavellian scheming of the father, who seems to regret what he has so carelessly inaugurated, is of powerful interest. The fine steadfast character of Peggy Haslam lightens the darker shadows of the book.

CPSIA information can be obtained
at www.ICGtesting.com
Printed in the USA
BVHW041354181118
533439BV00008B/61/P